Michael & Sue Price

# Internet
# for Seniors

Fourth Edition

In easy steps is an imprint of In Easy Steps Limited
4 Chapel Court · 42 Holly Walk · Leamington Spa
Warwickshire · United Kingdom · CV32 4YS
www.ineasysteps.com

Fourth Edition

Notice of Liability
Every effort has been made to ensure that this book contains accurate
and current information. However, In Easy Steps Limited and the
author shall not be liable for any loss or damage suffered by readers
as a result of any information contained herein.

Trademarks
Microsoft® and Windows® are registered trademarks of Microsoft
Corporation. All other trademarks are acknowledged as belonging to
their respective companies.

In Easy Steps Limited supports The Forest Stewardship Council (FSC),
the leading international forest certification organisation. All our titles
that are printed on Greenpeace approved FSC certified paper carry the
FSC logo.

**MIX**
Paper from
responsible sources
**FSC**
www.fsc.org   FSC® C020837

Printed and bound in the United Kingdom

ISBN  978-1-84078-577-7

# Contents

## 9 Digital Photography 131

## 10 For the Grandchildren 145

# 1 Get Started

This chapter outlines the Internet and the World Wide Web, it discusses the facilities you need to get on the Internet from your computer, and introduces Internet Explorer and the alternative browsers that give you safe and secure access to the Internet.

# The Internet

The Internet (Interconnected Network) is a global network connecting millions of computers, organized into thousands of commercial, academic, domestic and government networks located in over 100 countries. The Internet is sometimes called the Information Highway, because it provides the transportation and routing for the information exchanged between the connected computers.

The computers on the Internet are connected by a variety of methods, including the telephone system, wired networks, wireless (radio) networks, cable TV and even satellite.

**Beware**

There is no overseer, or manager, for the Internet, so Internet security is provided by software installed on your computer (see page 214).

**Hot tip**

The computers on the Internet are known as hosts or servers, and they create exchanges for news, views and data of all kinds.

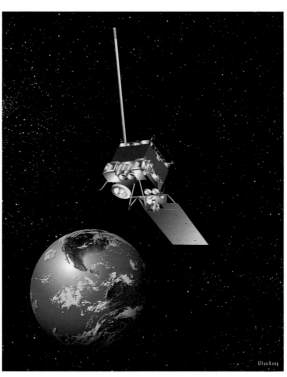

Some sections are commercial, others are academic or government, but no single organization owns the Internet as a whole. It is simply made up of individual, independent networks and computers, whose owners and operators decide which Internet methods to use and which local services to offer to the global Internet community.

# Internet Services

The services offered could include one or more of these:

- **Electronic mail (email)**

  This allows you and other Internet users to send and receive messages.

- **FTP (File Transfer Protocol)**

  This allows your computer to retrieve files from a remote computer and view or save them onto your computer.

- **Internet Service Providers (ISPs)**

  These, as the name suggests, provide points of access to the Internet. You need an ISP account, plus the means of connecting your computer to one of their computers.

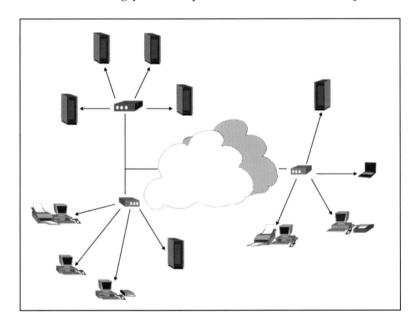

- **World Wide Web (WWW)**

  Also known as the Web, this is made up of collections of files and documents that may include images, animation, video and hyperlinks to other documents. These can be on the same computer, or on different computers, anywhere on the Internet.

**Don't forget**

There are other ways to connect to the Internet that don't require a computer, such as by cellphone, or a PDA device.

**Don't forget**

A location on the Web is known as a website. It will have a home page, the document that you see when you enter the site. It might have additional documents (web pages) and files, usually related to the main theme or focus.

**Hot tip**

To visit a website, and follow the hyperlinks in the web pages, you will need an Internet browser (see page 17).

11

# Requirements

To connect to the Internet, there are a number of things that you'll require:

**1** A computer equipped for use on the Internet. In this book we assume that you are using a Windows-based PC (see page 13)

**2** A means of connecting your PC (or PCs) to the computers at your ISP, including the hardware components, the communications software and the cabling, or phone links

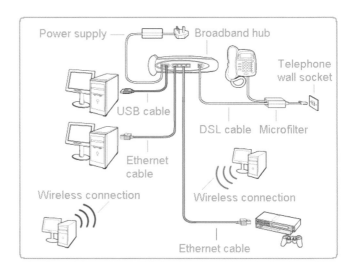

**3** An ISP account that will provide access to the Internet. You may also need email services, which would normally use the same account

**4** Appropriate software on your computer, to exchange information with other computers on the Internet, and to send and receive emails

We'll look at each of these in turn, so you will know all the tasks that are involved in setting up your computer, and can identify what remains to be done.

12

# Internet Enabled Computer

If you purchased your computer within the last three or four years, it will almost certainly be adequate for most activities on the Internet. If you have an older computer, review these hardware and software specifications to see if it will meet your needs for Internet access.

### Processor

If your computer has a Pentium 1GHz processor, or anything faster than this, you won't be restricted by the power of your computer.

### Operating System

While any version of Windows will allow you to access the Internet, for the best security you should upgrade to Windows 7 or later. The Home Premium and Ultimate editions are recommended for home users, and Professional or Enterprise for businesses.

### Memory

Although it is possible to run your computer with less memory, your use of the Internet will be smoother and more effective if you have memory of 2GB or more installed.

### Hard Disk Drive

Check the free space on your hard drive. If there is 20GB or more available, you'll have no problems with disk space. Any less, and you might wish to consider replacing the drive, or simply adding a second drive.

### Display Monitor and Adapter

To take full advantage of the Internet, you should preferably have a 17" monitor or larger, capable of displaying Hicolor (16bit), Trucolor (24bit) or better, at a resolution of 1024 x 768 pixels. For high definition videos, a wide screen with up to 1920 x 1080 pixels would be recommended.

**Don't forget**

Other requirements include a soundcard, speakers and DVD drive, if you want to play videos on your computer. You may also want a printer, and perhaps a scanner, but these are not essential for accessing the Internet.

**Hot tip**

To check the computer specifications, open Control Panel, click System and Maintenance and then System, to see the operating system level, the processor type and the memory installed.

**Don't forget**

Open the Computer folder and select the individual drive to check the size and the space available on that drive, displayed in the Details panel at the foot of the window.

# Connection Types

The type of connection you need depends on how much use you will be making of Internet access. There are four main options, though not all are available in every region.

Hot tip

You may pay as you go, for the call or connection time, or pay a fixed fee for a specified maximum number of hours, depending on which works out most economical for your average amount of usage.

### Dial-up
This is a low speed, low cost method for limited usage (less than say, five hours per week). It uses a Modem in your computer, which connects to a standard telephone socket. Your normal phone line is unavailable for incoming or outgoing calls while you are using the Internet.

### ADSL Broadband
This offers higher speed and supports a higher level of usage. It uses an ADSL modem attached to your computer or, alternatively, a separate device known as a router. It makes use of your telephone connection, but transfers data in a digital format that allows the line to remain available for normal incoming or outgoing calls. You can, if you wish, leave your computer connected all the time.

### Cable TV
If your area has Cable TV services, these may offer a broadband connection. This operates in a similar fashion to ADSL Broadband, but is independent of your telephone line.

### Satellite
If there are no ADSL or cable services available in your area, satellite services can provide you with a permanent two-way connection to the Internet that uses no telephone line. All you need is an interface box, and a small satellite dish connected to your computer. There are services designed for home use, a local community or businesses.

Beware

You may have a Wireless connection with ADSL Broadband. This still uses the normal telephone cables to connect to the ISP, but allows you to access the router from anywhere in your home. However, this is not full wireless connection.

### Wireless
This is the type of connection you use with a laptop computer (or a handheld unit) when you are away from home, at an airport, hotel or Internet cafe. Your computer will have a wireless modem, and the organization that you are visiting will provide the wireless access point which, in turn, connects to the Internet.

# ISP Account

Having decided on the type of connection that meets your needs, you need an Internet Service Provider to complete the connection. There are several ways to identify ISPs:

- Ask friends and family which ISP they use

- Check for pre-installed links on your computer for setting up a well-known ISP, such as AOL or MSN

- Look for CDs for ISPs, in the information supplied with your computer, to get onscreen instructions

- Check at your local bookstore, supermarket or computer store, for ISP CDs and special offers

If you have access to the Internet on another system, visit a website that can help you choose a suitable service. For example, to choose a broadband service:

**1** Go to www.theispguide.com/ for details of North American providers

**2** Search in your location by specifying the Area Code, or City and State

15

**Don't forget**

Check that your selected ISP will provide a modem, router or other hardware components that are needed to set up your broadband account.

**Don't forget**

There are similar ISP lists available for other regions and countries.

**Hot tip**

ISPs for the UK and Australia can also be listed with this guide.

# Set Up Internet Connection

## Don't forget

There's usually a setup CD, available from your ISP, that will take you, step by step, through the connection process, with explanations at each stage. This will avoid setting up your connection manually.

## Hot tip

In this example, a dial-up network connection for NetZero is being set up. This provides a dial-up service that is free apart from the telephone line charges. This could be useful as a backup, or for lower levels of usage.

In most cases, the instructions you require to set up and configure your Internet connection will be made available by the Internet Service Provider you have selected. However, Windows does provide guidance for creating the connection. This may be useful when you are setting up, for example, a simple dial-up connection, perhaps using the ISP account from your previous computer. To run this wizard:

**1** Select Start, type network, and select Network and Sharing Center

**2** Select to Set up a new connection or network

**3** Choose your required connection option, for example Dial-up, then click the Next button and enter the phone number, username and account password

**4** Click Connect to complete the connection setup

# Start your Browser

The first step in browsing the Internet is to start your Internet browser software. By default, this will be Internet Explorer, though you can choose an alternative (see page 19). There are two methods that you might use:

**1** Click Start, All Programs, and then select your browser from the Start menu

**2** If the browser has been pinned to the taskbar, select its icon

In either case, the browser will be opened. If it is not already active, your connection to the Internet will be established. When the connection completes, the default web page, in this case Google.com, will be displayed.

This is known as your Home page, and it appears whenever you start your browser, or press the Home button on the toolbar. The page address is specified when your software is installed or re-configured, and is usually a news page chosen by your ISP. However, you can select the web page (or web pages) that you'd prefer (see page 34).

**Hot tip**

To add your browser to the taskbar, right-click its entry in the Start menu and select Pin to Taskbar.

17

**Hot tip**

Default means a particular value or setting (in this case a web page) that is assigned automatically, and remains in effect until you cancel or change it.

# Internet Explorer Window

Your browser is the key component in any Internet activity, so you should become familiar with all of its features.

Title bar

Back button

Home button

Command bar

Web Page Window

Address bar    Current tab    New tab button

**National Trust Historic Sites**

## Treasured Connections
Each National Trust Historic Site keeps part of our history alive. Help support them >

PHOTO COURTESY CAROL M. HIGHSMIT

Status bar                              Scroll bars    Zoom

To add extra buttons, or to remove buttons, from the toolbar:

 Right-click the toolbar, select Customize, and then Add or Remove Commands

Press the Alt key to display the Menu bar temporarily, or right click the toolbar and select Menu Bar to display it continually.

File   Edit   View   Favorites   Tools   Help

Menu Bar
✓  Favorites Bar
   Compatibility View Button
✓  Command Bar
✓  Status Bar
   Windows Live Toolbar
✓  Lock the Toolbars
   Customize

✓  Use Large Icons
   Show Stop and Refresh Buttons before Address Bar
   Show All Text Labels
●  Show Selective Text
   Show Only Icons
   Add or Remove Commands...

 Select a toolbar button and click Add or Remove, as appropriate

Customize Toolbar

Available toolbar buttons:                    Current toolbar buttons:                Close

Encoding                                       Home                                     Reset
Edit                          Add ->           Feeds
Cut                           <- Remove        Read Mail
Copy                                           Print                                    Move Up
Paste                                          Page                                     Move Down

# Other Browser Software

The browser supplied with Windows is Internet Explorer; the version depends on which release of Windows you have. However, there are alternative browsers. To view the main browsers for Windows versions, type www.browserchoice.eu into the address bar and press Enter.

**Don't forget**

Within Europe, Microsoft offers a Browser choice via Windows Update, to give a choice of browsers that could replace the supplied Internet Explorer.

**①** Select the Download link for one of the browsers for your operating system, e.g. Mozilla Firefox and follow the prompts to install the selected browser

**②** When you start the new browser, you'll be asked if you want to make it the new default for web pages

**Hot tip**

The Update will put a shortcut to the Browser Choice on your desktop, or, in Windows 8, add a tile. You do not have to choose immediately. Internet Explorer will still be available on your system, but the Internet Explorer icon will disappear from the Taskbar and will need to be re-pinned. See page 17.

**③** Click No to keep Internet Explorer as the default. You are able to install a number of browsers on your system, but one of them will be specified as the default web browser

# Alternative Browsers

**Don't forget**

With an alternative browser, there are differences in icons, images and terms, but the functions are similar, and you'll still be able to take advantage of the suggestions and examples in this book.

**Hot tip**

These browsers use the term Bookmarks, rather than Favorites, and have Google, rather than Bing, as the default search engine.

**Hot tip**

Over the last few years, the Google Chrome browser has been growing substantially in popularity – it's renowned for faster browsing.

**1** This shows the Opera browser, with the same set of web pages shown for Internet Explorer (see page 18)

**2** This shows the Mozilla Firefox browser, again with the same set of web pages displayed

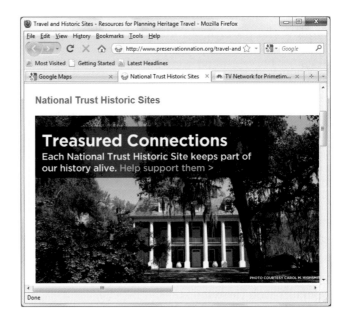

# 2 Browse the Internet

*The Internet is an enormous library of information, but it is not at all organized. So you have to locate what you need by name, through links or by searching using descriptive keywords, taking full advantage of the capabilities of your browsing software.*

# Web Page Address

To find your way around the Internet, you need to understand web page addresses. For example, the sample home page (see page 17) has this web address:

| 8 http://www.**google.com**/index.html    🔎 ▾ ⟳ ✕ |

This address is made up of several parts:

- http:// — Indicates web pages
- www.google.com — The web server name
- index.html — The web page name

The web server name is, itself, made up of several parts:

- www — Indicates a host computer
- google — The company or owner name
- com — The website type

You will encounter various other website types, such as:

- com — Commercial website
- org — Organization – usually nonprofit
- edu — Education (e.g. university)
- gov — Government department

There are international versions of these website types, incorporating a country identification, for example:

- com.au, org.au, edu.au, gov.au — Australia
- co.in, org.in, ac.in, gov.in — India
- co.uk, org.uk, ac.uk, gov.uk — United Kingdom

There are also various website types that are not associated with any particular country:

- biz, info, me, net — Business related

(see page 17)

**Don't forget**

The web server name incorporates the Domain name, which consists of owner name and website type, in this case google.com. Other examples of domain names are: microsoft.com preservationnation.org

**Beware**

Individuals, as well as companies, can register domain names of many different types, so the name itself does not tell you anything about the owner.

**Hot tip**

Although there are general similarities, the naming is not entirely consistent, country to country, e.g. using co instead of com, and ac (Academic) instead of edu.

# Open a Web Page

If you find a web page address in an article or advertisement, or are given a web address by a friend, you can direct the browser to display that page. For example, to display the World of Playing Cards web page, www.wopc.co.uk:

**1** Start Internet Explorer and click the address bar area. The address is highlighted

**2** Type the required web page address. This replaces the existing highlighted address

**3** Press Enter to display the required page

**4** You may see a progress indicator on the Status bar, depending on how quickly the web page loads

**Hot tip**

As you type, Internet Explorer suggests possible values that may complete the address, without you having to enter the complete value.

**Hot tip**

You do not need to type the http:// part of a web address. Internet Explorer inserts it automatically.

**Don't forget**

Web pages often feature banner adverts at the top, and spot adverts on the sides. These encourage you to visit the site sponsors. However, you are under no obligation to do so.

**Hot tip**

You can zoom in to enlarge text and images. See page 46 for instructions on how to do this.

# Links

When you've displayed one web page, you can usually go on to another page without having to type a web page address. Instead, you click on items on the current page that have web addresses associated with them. These items are called Links (or Hyperlinks). They are often descriptive text, underlined and colored blue, or red, as in the example.

To confirm whether a part of the page is a link:

1 Place the mouse pointer over the item. If it is a link, the pointer changes to a hand symbol, to indicate that there is a link address

2 The target location is shown on the status bar

3 Sometimes the link is associated with a graphic image, and again the pointer changes to a hand

4 The image may also have a descriptive Tool Tip

# Follow Links

**1** Click the Alphabetical Index of Card Games link at www.pagat.com to show the A to Z web page

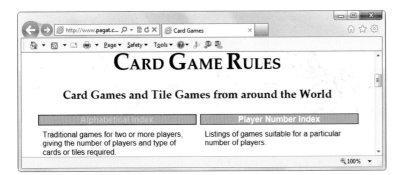

**Don't forget**

A link can point to a web page on a different site, or a web page on the same site, or a different location within the web page (as indicated by the #label appended to the web page address).

**2** Click the M link to move down the same web page to the location www.pagat.com/alpha.html#m

**Hot tip**

The slider on the scroll bar indicates where you are on the page. You can click and drag this slider to reposition your view.

**3** Click any link to visit that web page, where you will find information about the game's history, websites to visit and further useful links

When you visit a location, the color of the link changes, typically from blue to purple, providing a visual cue for future visits, to remind you that you have previously followed that particular link.

**Don't forget**

The hyperlink color will remain changed, even when you restart Internet Explorer, until you clear the browsing history, or the records expire.

# Address Help

Internet Explorer offers you help with entering web page addresses, in several ways.

This shows the most recent web pages at the top. When you select an entry, it appears on the address bar, so you can modify it if necessary. Then press Enter or click the blue button.

**1** Click the arrow at the end of the Address bar, to see a list of web page addresses that you have typed previously, and click the one that you want

In this case, selecting an entry takes you to that web page. There's no need to press Enter.

**2** If you start typing an address, Internet Explorer lists previously-visited web pages that match the part entered so far. As soon as you see the required web page, click the entry to open it

Internet Explorer adds the prefix http://www and the suffix com, then attempts to display that location.

**3** Type the company, or organization, name on the address bar, and then press Ctrl + Enter. For example:

will display

Even if this gives the wrong address, the organization may intercept it and offer the correct address.

# Add to Favorites

When you visit a web page that you find useful, make it easy to find at another time by adding it to your list of favorites.

**1** While viewing the web page, click the Favorites button and then click Add to Favorites

**2** The title of the page is suggested as the name, or you can type another, perhaps more descriptive, name

**3** Click Add to put the page details onto the main list

**4** Click the Favorites button and select the Favorites tab to display the list

**5** Select any page you wish to visit (click the blue arrow to open a new tab for the page)

## Hot tip

Pages you visit every day can become your home page, so they open whenever Internet Explorer opens. See page 17.

## Don't forget

Press the New Folder button to create a subfolder in the Favorites list. Click the down-arrow to select a subfolder in which to store the web page details.

## Hot tip

If you forgot to add a web page, and you want to find it again, click the History tab and you'll see the pages you have visited over a recent period of time.

# Searching

If you have no idea of the correct website, Internet Explorer will carry out a search on your behalf.

**1** Click the magnifying glass in the Address box. This changes the function to a Search facility and removes the existing text

**2** Type some appropriate keywords and press Enter. Internet Explorer uses your default search engine to find web pages related to your search terms

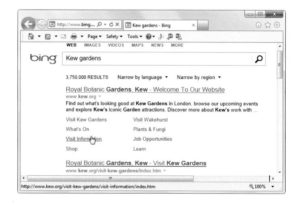

**3** Scroll down or page forward until you find the website you want, then click the header

**4** Press the Back button to return to the search results

# Add Search Providers

If you prefer to use different search providers, you can make additional providers available, and change the default.

**1** Click the down arrow in the Address box (Show Address Bar Autocomplete), and select Add, to open the Internet Explorer Add-ons Gallery

**2** Select Search Provider and click your choice from the list of recommended providers

**3** Click the button to Add to Internet Explorer

**4** Click the box to Make this my default search provider, if required, and then click the Add button

**5** In future sessions you could select your search provider from the icons at the bottom of the drop-down Address box

## Hot tip

Select other countries and languages from the top of the Gallery to display the associated search providers. The default is the location you specify in the Control Panel, e.g. United States (English).

## Hot tip

You can select a specific Search Provider for particular sessions, for example, checking security issues and hoax emails.

## Don't forget

Select Tools, Manage Add-ons and Search providers, to disable search suggestions, change the listing order, remove an entry or set a new default.

# Specific Searches

**Don't forget**

You could target your search towards videos, shopping, news or maps, instead of web pages or images.

1 By default, searches will be for relevant web pages

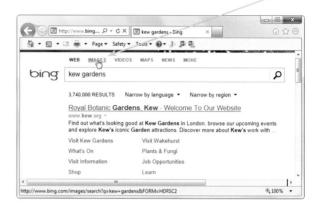

2 Click Images to search for relevant images, which will be displayed as thumbnails

**Hot tip**

Click the triangle next to Size, to control the results by image size. You can also choose layout, color, style or people attributes.

3 Click a thumbnail and select Full-size to view the image, or right-click and choose Save picture as, to capture a copy

See full size image (660 × 495 · 71kB · jpeg)

# Open New Tab

Tabs allow you to have more than one web page open at the same time, without having to open a separate copy of your browser. To open a new tab:

**1** Click New Tab on the tab row (or press Ctrl + T)

**2** A New Tab opens, with recently-visited sites suggested for immediate selection

**3** Reopen tabs that you have previously closed, in the current session. Click the down arrow to see a list

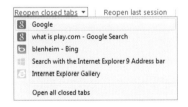

**4** You can also Reopen the last browsing session from this window. This action leaves your current tabs available and adds the previous tabs to the tab line

**Don't forget**

Sometimes when you click on a link in a web page, the link will automatically open on a new tab. The back button will not be active, and you will need to close the tab to return to the previous web page.

**Hot tip**

You can turn on InPrivate Browsing, which lets you surf the Internet without leaving traces, by automatically clearing your web history when you close the session.

**31**

**Don't forget**

The title for each page appears on the appropriate tab.

# Using Tabs

There are several more ways for you to specify a new web page and open it in a new tab.

1. Type the web page location on the address bar, with the current tab displayed, then press Alt + Enter. This opens the required address on a new tab

2. Right-click a hyperlink on the web page and select to Open in New tab

3. Hold down the Ctrl key as you left-click a hyperlink on the web page

4. Hover over the Internet Explorer button on the Taskbar to get an instant thumbnail view of open tabs

**Hot tip**

Click Tools and select Reopen last browsing session to open previously-active tabs.

**Hot tip**

When Quick tabs are active, press Ctrl + Q to display thumbnails of open tabs.

5. Move the mouse over the thumbnail to get a full window. Click to select an individual tab

6. To enable Quick Tabs, as seen in previous versions of Internet Explorer, select Tools, Internet options, Tab settings and tick the box to Enable Quick Tabs

# Close Tabs

Having opened a number of tabs, you can close them individually or all at once.

**1** Click the X on the currently-selected tab (or press Ctrl + W) to close that tab

**2** Right-click any tab and select Close Tab

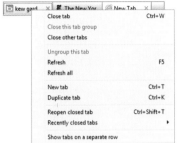

**3** Select Close Other Tabs (and leave the selected tab open)

**4** If you change your mind, select Reopen Closed Tab to open the last one closed, or select Recently Closed Tabs to select one from the list

**5** You can refresh the selected tab, (press F5), or all tabs or duplicate the tab

**6** Click the Close button (or press Alt + F4) to close Internet Explorer

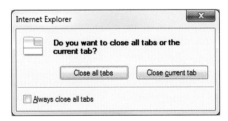

**7** Select Close all tabs, and end the browsing session

**8** You can Reopen Last Browsing Session when you select New Tab (see page 31) the next time you open Internet Explorer

**Don't forget**

You must have previously enabled Quick tabs, as on the previous page, to close a tab group or ungroup tabs.

**33**

**Hot tip**

To save all open tabs, and make them available for reloading as a group, click Favorites, click the arrow next to Add to Favorites (see page 27) and select Add Current Tabs to Favorites.

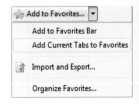

# Change Home Page

You can change the web page used as the initial page when Internet Explorer starts up.

## Hot tip

If you find a web page that would make a good home page, you can specify it to add to, or replace, the one that is currently defined.

 Open your preferred web page, PBS TV for example, by typing its URL on the address bar (see page 23)

 At www.pbs.org, click the arrow next to the Home Page button

 Select the option to Add or Change Home Page

## Don't forget

Select Use this web page as your only home page, to replace the existing home page with the currently-displayed web page.

**34**

 Choose an option, for example, Use this web page as your only home, and click Yes to apply the change

The specified web page opens automatically when you click the Home button, or whenever you start Internet Explorer.

### Blank Home Page

If you decide that you do not require a home page at all:

## Hot tip

If there are multiple home page tabs, you can selectively remove some of them.

 Display the Home page menu and select Remove, Remove All, then Yes to confirm

From now on, a blank web page is displayed when you start Internet Explorer, or press the Home button.

# 3 Puzzles and Solutions

*Use online reference materials to look up words, get solutions to crossword clues, locate facts or resolve anagrams. You can also use the Internet as a source of entertaining puzzles and quizzes, or to locate online books, especially the classics, which you can read and research.*

# Solve Crosswords

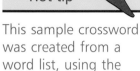
You might make a start by using the Internet to help you with a crossword. Suppose you have a partially-solved crossword, and want to use the Internet to help complete it:

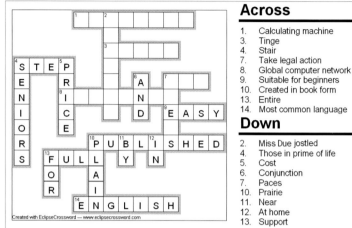

**Across**

1.  Calculating machine
3.  Tinge
4.  Stair
7.  Take legal action
8.  Global computer network
9.  Suitable for beginners
10. Created in book form
13. Entire
14. Most common language

**Down**

2.  Miss Due jostled
4.  Those in prime of life
5.  Cost
6.  Conjunction
7.  Paces
10. Prairie
11. Near
12. At home
13. Support

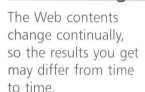
 Click the magnifying glass in the Address box to modify it for searching and type the keywords solve crossword and click the arrow

2 The website at www.oneacross.com offers free help with crosswords (and anagrams and cryptograms)

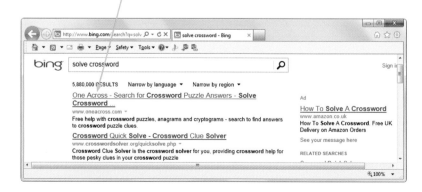

# Resolve Clues

The OneAcross website allows you to enter complete clues, along with the number of letters required. For example:

**1** Type the clue Take legal action and the pattern ??? (meaning three letters, all unknown), and click Go!

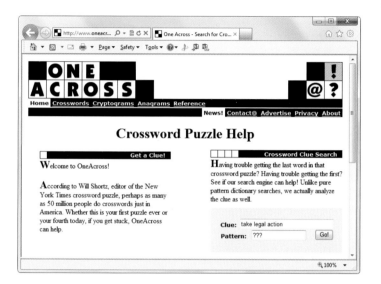

**2** The website displays the answers that it finds, with the most likely answer shown first

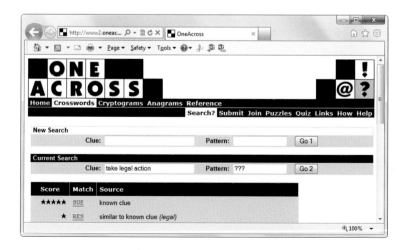

# Find Anagrams

Many crosswords incorporate anagrams in the clues. The server at www.wordsmith.org/anagram helps with these.

Solve clue 2 down: Miss Due jostled(7).

1. Type the anagram word or phrase (spaces will be ignored), e.g. miss due, and click Get Anagrams

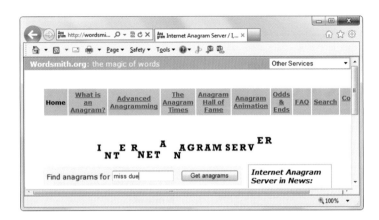

Words, such as Jostle, Transform or Sort, are used in clues to indicate that the remaining words form an anagram to be solved.

2. The website displays all the answers that it can find. These can include multiple words, abbreviations, acronyms etc.

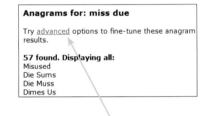

**Anagrams for: miss due**

Try advanced options to fine-tune these anagram results.

**57 found. Displaying all:**
Misused
Die Sums
Die Muss
Dimes Us

3. For more specific answers, use the Advanced options

The Advanced options will allow you to specify the number of words, or the number of letters per word (minimum and maximum), and the language. You can also specify words that must be included, if you've partially solved the anagram.

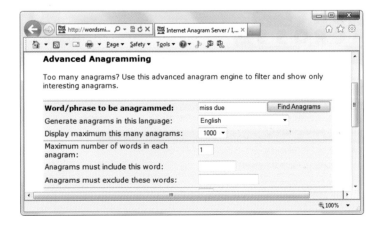

# Look Up Words

You can look up words in an online dictionary, for example:

**1**   Visit www.onelook.com, and type the pattern for the word, using ???s and inserting letters you know

Hot tip

Solve clue 1 across: Calculating machine(8).

**2**   OneLook defaults to All Matches, and lists the potential answers in alphabetic order

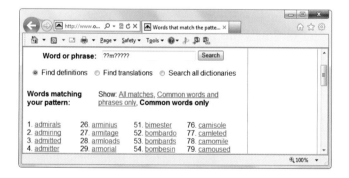

Hot tip

If there are many possibilities, only the first 100 are listed. Select Common Words Only, to reduce the number.

**3**   Add words from the clue (separated by a colon from the word pattern). The most likely will be listed first

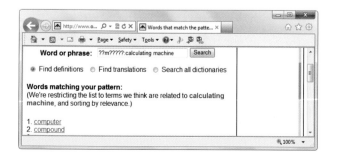

Beware

Words from the clue may not help if you are completing a cryptic crossword, since they may not appear in the literal definitions.

# Crosswords Online

The Internet doesn't just help you solve crosswords, it is also a rich source of crosswords. You will soon find your own favorite sites, but to help get you started, try one of the newspapers. For example:

**1** Type games.washingtonpost.com/ on the address bar and press Enter to open the web page

**2** Scroll down the page to locate the Daily crossword, select a date and choose Play Regular or Play Master

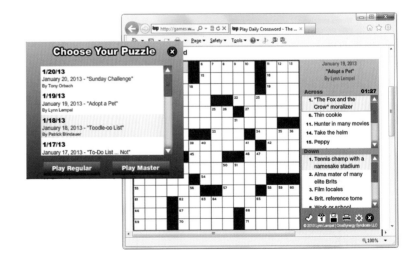

**3** The full crossword will be displayed with clues and the option to Save or Print

# Interactive Crosswords

You can complete the crosswords interactively.

**1** Select the crossword you want to complete

**2** If Java isn't already installed, you may get a warning message

**3** Select More Info and follow the prompts to go to www.java.com and download the required version

**4** You can now enter the solutions on the screen

**Hot tip**

You'll need the Java software installed on your computer to access most dynamic web sites, games and utilities.

**Hot tip**

You may also be prompted to install the free Flash Player from Adobe Macromedia.

**Don't forget**

You can Save your solution periodically, and click the Solve icon to get help for individual letters, words or to complete the whole puzzle for you. Incorrect letters are marked in red.

# Sudoku

If you want a change from crosswords, you might switch to Sudoku. The Internet will provide advice and suggestions for completing the puzzles you find in magazines, and offer puzzles for you to play online or to print out to complete later.

**1** Go to www.websudoku.com which claims to have billions of Sudoku puzzles for you to play

**Hot tip**

Click Select a puzzle, and specify the level, then go to a puzzle at random, or enter the specific number to repeat a previous puzzle.

Level: Easy ▾
Number: 123456
Leave blank to select a random puzzle.
Go to this puzzle

**2** Click an empty cell and type a suitable digit, based on the contents of other cells. Your entries are shown in blue italics

**Don't forget**

Click Options to set the timer, to change the strictness of the progress report, or to allow you to pencil in multiple possibilities in a cell.

**3** To check your progress, click How am I doing? You'll be warned if you've entered a wrong number

# Solving Puzzles

Here are some useful websites that explain some of the techniques involved in solving Sudoku puzzles.

**1** At www.simetric.co.uk/sudoku you'll find three tutorials that demonstrate solving Sudoku puzzles

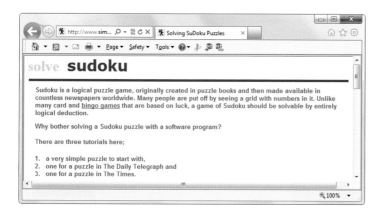

**2** There's a comprehensive guide to solving Sudoku, at www.sudoku.org.uk/PDF/Solving_Sudoku.pdf

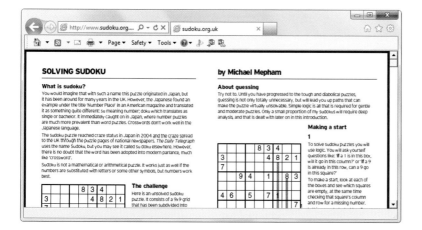

**3** Finally, for the count of valid Sudoku grids, see www.afjarvis.staff.shef.ac.uk/sudoku/sudoku.pdf

# Brain Aerobics

Brain teasers, quizzes and games are not just for fun, or to pass the time, they also provide essential mental exercise.

**1** Search for brain teasers for seniors to find sites, such as www.clevelandseniors.com/forever/mindex.htm

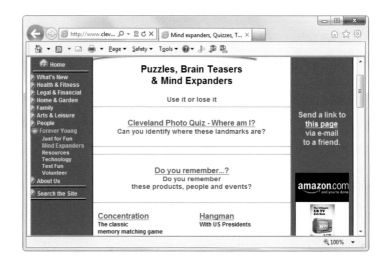

**2** Select one of the 25 or so links of Mind Expanders, for example Concentration or Trivia & Quizzes

**3** If you want more cerebral exercise, visit the website www.mensa.org and click Mensa Workout

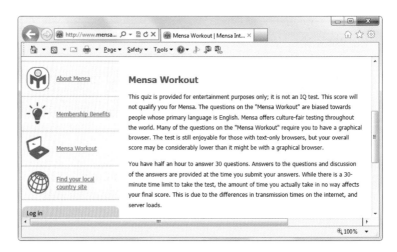

# Web Encyclopedia

To help you answer all the quizzes you find, you'll need good reference material. Make a start with the web encyclopedia that you can edit and update, as well as reference.

1.  Go to www.wikipedia.org and choose your preferred language

2.  Click Log in/create account to specify your username, password and (optionally) email address

3.  Explore the articles. Search for topics, or just click the Random Article link to see what appears

4.  Select Main page, and scroll down to list the user-maintained sister projects

**Don't forget**

Wikipedia is hosted by the Wikimedia Foundation, a non-profit organization that also hosts a range of other projects.

**Don't forget**

It isn't essential to create an account, but it does let you communicate with other Wikipedia users.

**Beware**

In principle, anybody can contribute to the Wikipedia projects. In practice, older articles tend to be more comprehensive and balanced, while newer articles may contain misinformation or unencyclopedic info, or even vandalism.

# Internet Public Library

## Hot tip

ipl2 provides an annotated collection of high quality Internet resources, selected by the IPL staff as providing accurate and factual information.

The Internet Public Library (ipl2), supported by the College of Information at Florida State University, offers information services to Internet users, helping them to find, evaluate and organize information.

1. Visit www.ipl.org to see subject collections, ready reference and reading room material etc.

2. ipl2 also offers to research individual questions for you if the question is considered suitable

## Don't forget

To change the screen resolution, right-click the desktop, select Screen resolution, click the down arrow next to Resolution and drag the Resolution slider.

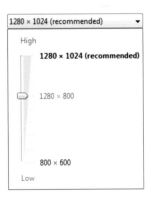

## Zoom

Reading text or articles online can be made easier by changing the screen resolution or zoom level on Internet Explorer.

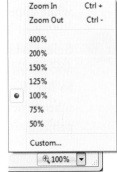

1. Click the Zoom button at the foot of the window, to switch between 100%, 125%, and 150%, and so enlarge the view

2. Click the down-arrow to choose a preset level, between 50% and 400%, or choose a Custom value

46

# Online Classics

You can find the full text for many thousands of books on the Internet, in an electronic (ebook) format that is ideal for searching for particular details. They are books whose copyright has expired, and, in the main, they are classics. There are online books on Wikipedia, and on ipl2, but perhaps the best source for free ebooks is Project Gutenberg.

**1** Type www.gutenberg.org and press Enter to display the home page for the website

**2** Click Online Book Catalog, to locate books by author or by title

**3** Click Recent Books, or Top 100, to view lists of books in those categories

**4** Advanced Search allows you to search for books with specific words or phrases in the text

**5** Project Gutenberg also covers a wide range of books in other languages

**Hot tip**

You can participate in Project Gutenberg, for example, by volunteering to proof read individual pages of books.

**Beware**

If you don't live in the US, you should check the copyright laws in your country before downloading an ebook.

47

**Don't forget**

You can also browse the database, arranged alphabetically by title or by author.

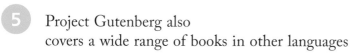

# Online Reference

When it's reference books you want, visit the Bartleby website, where you can access a wide range of well known books.

1. Go to www.bartleby.com and click the down-arrow next to the Search box to choose the specific type

2. Choose a book, by Subject, Title or Author, search a section (Reference, Verse, Fiction, or Non-fiction) or select Thesaurus, Quotations or English usage

3. When you select a specific book, the full text is provided for you to search, or read, online

4. The site also offers a link to free ebook downloads from the Amazon.com-enabled store

Bartleby
Bookstore

Buy the books published at Bartleby.com or download free e-books from the Amazon.com-enabled bookstore.

# 4 Chess and Bridge

*Even if you are home alone, you can participate in games of chess or bridge over the Internet. You can play against the computer, or against human opponents. You can watch others play, historical games or live events. You'll also get lots of help on the Internet to improve your game.*

# Chess Games

Chessgames.com is an online database of historic chess games that help chess players to develop their game.

## Hot tip

If Chess is your game, you can learn tricks and techniques by studying the games between the great masters, by searching at chessgames.com.

**1** To find a game, go to www.chessgames.com to display the home page, with several search options

## Beware

You can register free, but the site does offer premium memberships at a charge of $25 per annum, allowing you to use additional game analysis tools.

**2** Type a plain text game description in the search box, for example the player names, the year, and the opening move or the result, e.g. kasparov topalov 1-0

**3** Alternatively, fill in the fields on the Advanced Search form:
- Year
- Player
- White or Black
- Opposing player
- No. of moves
- Opening (name)
- ECO code
- Result

## Don't forget

You don't have to specify all the fields. In fact, most searches use just one or two fields to find games.

**50**

**4** Click the Find Chess Games button. The matching games will be listed. Click the game you want to see

# View Game

A chess board will be displayed, along with the list of moves that make up that particular game.

**1** Click any move to see the board configuration at that point in the game

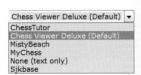

Beware

You'll need the Java software enabled (see page 41), and you may have to switch Java Viewers to find the one that works best on your system.

**2** Click the arrows to step forward or backward a move at a time, or to move to the start or end point

**3** Click the Guess the Move box to run the chess training, and take the part of a player

Hot tip

The games are stored using PGN (Portable Game Notation), a simple text format which you can download and import to Chess software running on your PC.

# Play the Computer

Studying chess games is educational, but you really need to play games in order to improve your skill level. There are many websites where you can play other people, friends or strangers, but perhaps you could start off by playing against a computer program, such as Little Chess Partner.

**1** Go to www.chessica.de/gamezone.html and click the first Play button, to play against the computer

**2** Click the board to start, then drag to move a (white) chess piece turn by turn. The computer won't let you make an illegal move

**3** Click the Settings button to change the thinking time, or the depth of analysis, used by the computer

# ...cont'd

If you find the Little Chess Partner too challenging, there's an easier program that you can play against, to get practice.

**1** Scroll down and click the link Try This!, which appears below the chess board display

**2** Choose Black or White for the computer, and then take your turn – select a piece (which changes to purple) then click the destination to make your move. Only legal moves are allowed

**3** The Game Log records all the moves made

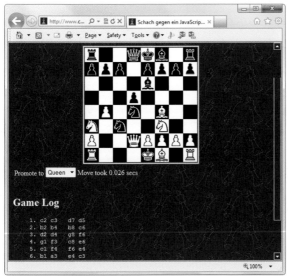

### Don't forget

The web author suggests, somewhat provocatively, that if you cannot beat this computer program, then perhaps you should try playing a different type of game.

**53**

### Hot tip

Select both Black and White for the CPU, and it will launch an automatic game, showing you the moves in the Log. Useful to get ideas for opening moves, but it usually ends in Stalemate, as you might expect.

# Chess Server

To introduce yourself to the world of chess on the Internet:

**1** Visit the Free Internet Chess Server (FICS) at www.freechess.org, to register for playing online

**2** Click the Download link to look for a graphical interface, the easiest way to connect to FICS

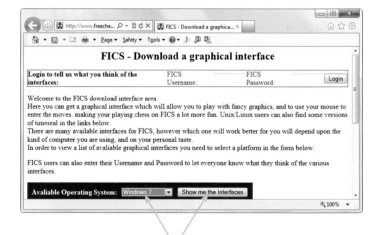

**3** Select operating system Windows 7 then click Show me the Interfaces

**4** Click an interface, for example: WinBoard by Tim Mann at http://www.tim-mann.org/xboard.html

# Graphical Interface

**1** Select XBoard and WinBoard, and follow the prompts to locate the download link for WinBoard

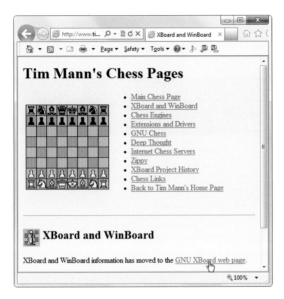

Hot tip

XBoard runs on Unix systems, while WinBoard runs on Windows. Tim Mann is the primary author of both applications.

**2** Follow the links to the GNU XBoard web page and select Winboard Forum, the Winboard Downloads and the WinBoard Installer program

Don't forget

WinBoard will be set as the viewer for .PGN files (Portable Game Notation – see page 51) and for .FEN files (Forsyth-Edwards Notation), another file type used for defining games.

# Chess Tournaments

At the Free Internet Chess Server there is a list of tournaments around the globe. You can keep up-to-date with the games of the Grand Masters and watch video of interviews with the various personalities.

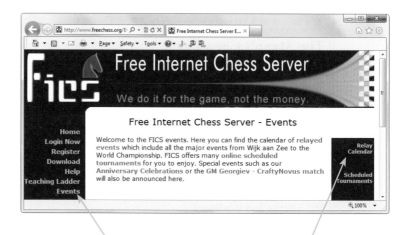

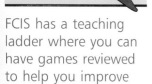

**1** Click the link to Events and then select Relay Calendar

**2** Choose the current year, and then a tournament that is actually taking place at the time – for example the Tata Steel Chess Tournament in the Netherlands

3    Click the link to Tata Steel Chess, the sponsor, and you are offered a variety of options, including live games and live video from the room itself

4    The main tournament page includes articles, comments and a competition

5    Click the Tournament tab to see completed games, illustrated step by step

### Hot tip

FCIS has its own website tournament in which you can participate. Events occur on a regular basis and scores and rankings are recorded. Click the link Scheduled Tournaments on the Events page.

# Bridge Online

**Don't forget**

There are eight zones in the World Bridge Federation:
1 Europe
2 North America
3 South America
4 Asia & Middle East
5 Central America & Caribbean
6 Pacific Asia
7 South Pacific
8 Africa

**Hot tip**

There are also links to bridge clubs, personal pages, youth bridge and commercial services.

If bridge is your game, it is well supported on the Internet, with many websites offering help and information. You might start with the World Bridge Federation website.

1 Visit www.worldbridge.org and click the Links entry

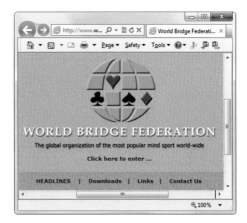

2 Select Official Organizations and choose the zone for your region to locate the national organization

3 Select Education from the Link Sections for useful resources identified by country and language

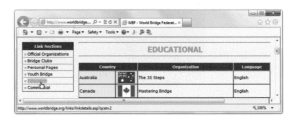

The national organizations also offer useful facilities. The EBU (English Bridge Union), for example, runs the Really Easy Bridge programme, featuring news and events that are designed to help beginners develop their bridge.

4 Visit www.reallyeasybridge.com to explore the options at the Really Easy Bridge website

5 Select the Point Count Table for a comprehensive analysis of opening, responses and rebids

6 Select the Revision Pages link for details on topics, such as Stayman

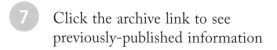

7 Click the archive link to see previously-published information

59

# Great Bridge Links

For a more international view of bridge, you'll find an organized list of bridge-related websites at the nicely named Great Bridge Links.

**1** Visit the website www.greatbridgelinks.com

**2** Click Bridge Campus for links to websites that will help you learn (or teach) the game of bridge

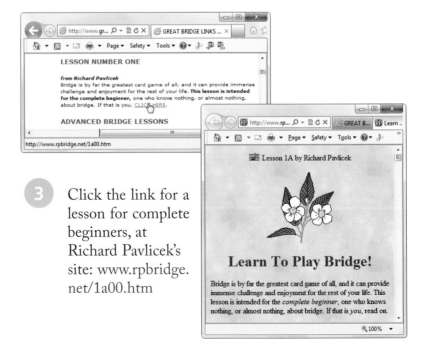

**3** Click the link for a lesson for complete beginners, at Richard Pavlicek's site: www.rpbridge.net/1a00.htm

Richard Pavlicek provides a complete teaching website, at www.rpbridge.net/, with basic and advanced bridge lessons.

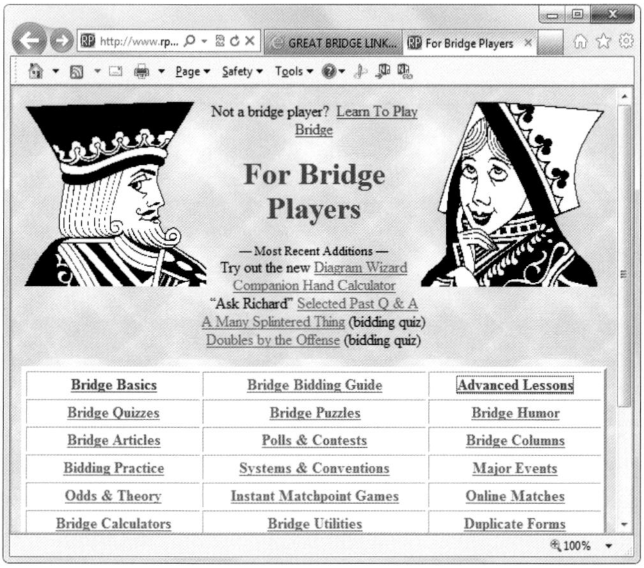


**Don't forget**

The Bridge Basics have 12 progressive lessons, and a series of quizzes, while the Advanced Bridge Lessons offer 50 lessons and 150 exercises.

There are other comprehensive websites listed, for example:

1. Visit Karen's Bridge Library at home.comcast.net/~kwbridge/
   This site includes a page of "On-your-own" activities to build your skills

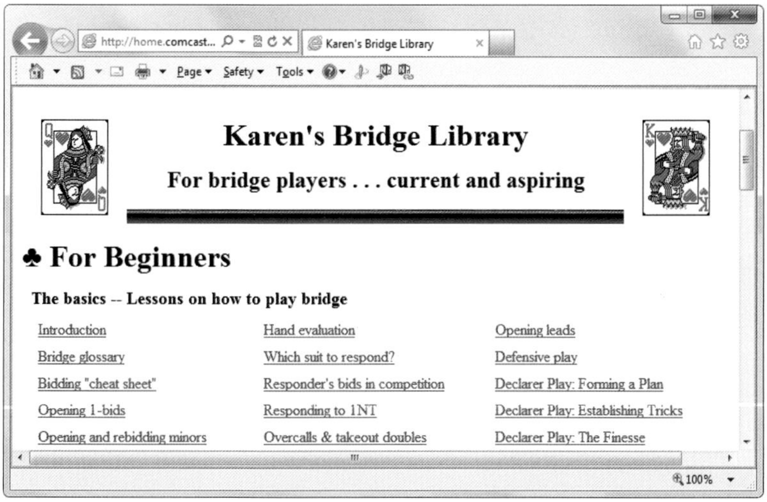


**Hot tip**

This website offers a collection of class handouts and reference sheets, suitable for beginner, intermediate and advanced players.

# Online Bridge Clubs

When you are ready to play Bridge online, you'll find numerous websites to help you get started and to find partners.

1 On the Great Bridge Links website, click the Play Online link for a list of online Bridge clubs

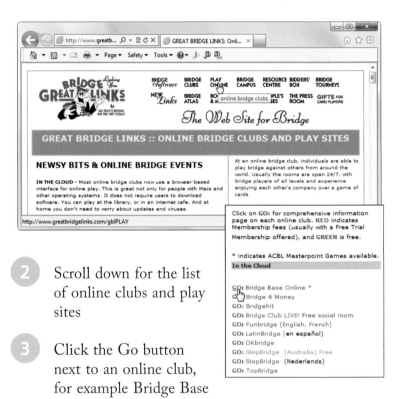

2 Scroll down for the list of online clubs and play sites

3 Click the Go button next to an online club, for example Bridge Base Online (BBO), to display the details for the club

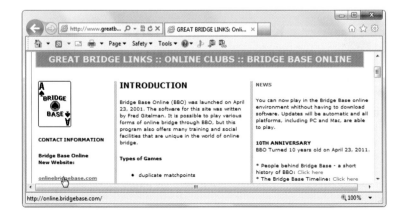

④ Click the website address provided, to visit the club

⑤ Select Vugraph Schedule to see the dates and times for tournament matches that will be broadcast

⑥ Click the link to view the archives of older matches

⑦ Selecting View for any match will display the scoreboard (see overleaf for an example)

**Don't forget**

You don't have to play bridge immediately. You can view current or recorded bridge games, using Vugraph broadcasts.

**Don't forget**

When you click a link on this website, the link automatically opens in a new tab or in a new window. In both cases, the Back button is not available and you must close the tab or window to return to the previous web page.

# View Bridge Games

**1** Open Bridge Base Online, and select a match from the Vugraph archives to display the scoreboard

This shows the results for all the games in the match, as played by each of the teams.

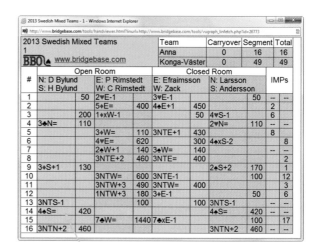

*2013 Swedish Mixed Teams - 1 - Windows Internet Explorer*

http://www.bridgebase.com/tools/handviewer.html?linurl=http://www.bridgebase.com/tools/vugraph_linfetch.php?id=26773

2013 Swedish Mixed Teams — 1 — BBO www.bridgebase.com

| Team | Carryover | Segment | Total |
|---|---|---|---|
| Anna | 0 | 16 | 16 |
| Konga-Väster | 0 | 49 | 49 |

| # | N: D Bylund / S: H Bylund | | E: P Rimstedt / W: C Rimstedt | | E: Efraimsson / W: Zack | | N: Larsson / S: Andersson | | IMPs | |
|---|---|---|---|---|---|---|---|---|---|---|
| | Open Room | | | | Closed Room | | | | | |
| 1 | | 50 | 2♥E-1 | | 3♥E-1 | | | 50 | -- | -- |
| 2 | | | 5♦E= | 400 | 4♠E+1 | 450 | | | 2 | |
| 3 | | 200 | 1♦xW-1 | | | 50 | 4♥S-1 | | 6 | |
| 4 | 3♠N= | 110 | | | 2♥N= | | | 110 | -- | -- |
| 5 | | | 3♦W= | 110 | 3NTE+1 | 430 | | | 8 | |
| 6 | | | 4♥E= | 620 | | 300 | 4♠xS-2 | | 8 | |
| 7 | | | 2♠W+1 | 140 | 3♠W= | 140 | | | -- | -- |
| 8 | | | 3NTE+2 | 460 | 3NTE= | 400 | | | 2 | |
| 9 | 3♦S+1 | 130 | | | | | 2♠S+2 | 170 | 1 | |
| 10 | | | 3NTW= | 600 | 3NTE-1 | 100 | | | 12 | |
| 11 | | | 3NTW+3 | 490 | 3NTW= | 400 | | | 3 | |
| 12 | | | 1NTW+3 | 180 | 3♦E-1 | 50 | | | 6 | |
| 13 | 3NTS-1 | | | 100 | | 100 | 3NTS-1 | | -- | -- |
| 14 | 4♠S= | 420 | | | 4♠S= | 420 | | | -- | -- |
| 15 | | | 7♠W= | 1440 | 7♠xE-1 | 100 | | | 17 | |
| 16 | 3NTN+2 | 460 | | | | | 3NTN+2 | 460 | -- | -- |

**2** Click an entry to display the hands for that game

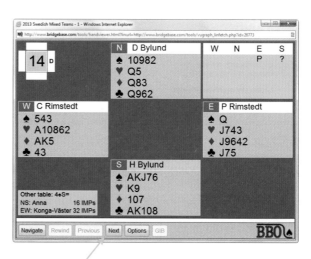

*2013 Swedish Mixed Teams - 1 - Windows Internet Explorer*

http://www.bridgebase.com/tools/handviewer.html?linurl=http://www.bridgebase.com/tools/vugraph_linfetch.php?id=26773

**14** D

| W | N | E | S |
|---|---|---|---|
| | | P | ? |

**N  D Bylund**
♠ 10982
♥ Q5
♦ Q83
♣ Q962

**W  C Rimstedt**
♠ 543
♥ A10862
♦ AK5
♣ 43

**E  P Rimstedt**
♠ Q
♥ J743
♦ J9642
♣ J75

**S  H Bylund**
♠ AKJ76
♥ K9
♦ 107
♣ AK108

Other table: 4♠S=
NS: Anna          16 IMPs
EW: Konga-Väster 32 IMPs

Navigate | Rewind | Previous | Next | Options | GIB       BBO

If you resize the window, the image of the board will be adjusted to fill the window, while maintaining the proportions.

**3** Click Next to view each stage in the bidding, and to show the cards as they are played

**4** Select Navigate to display the scoreboard, the next board or the other table

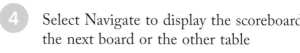

Scoreboard
Next board
Other table
Navigate

# Log in to BBO

**1** Open Bridge Base Online and select Play Bridge Now (see page 63)

**2** If registered, enter your user name and password and click Log in

**3** If not registered, click Become a member (free!)

**4** Provide a user name and password, and add the details you wish to record, then click OK

**5** When you've logged in, select Help me find a game

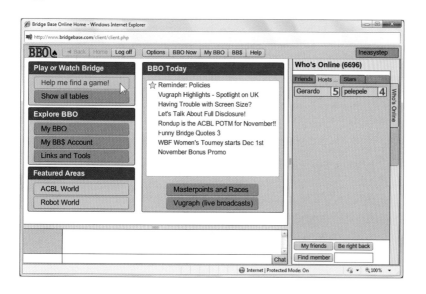

You will be able to watch games as an observer (see page 66), or join a table to play games yourself.

## Hot tip

You'll be told if your user name is already in use, so you can offer a new one.

That username is not available.

## Beware

The details you provide will be visible to all members, so provide limited information, until you are sure you want to remain as a member of BBO.

65

# Kibitz a Table

## Hot tip

If you don't feel ready to jump right in and join a table as a player, start by watching existing games.

## Don't forget

Players, or kibitzers, may chat using the message area at the foot of the window.

## Beware

Although BBO is free, some facilities, such as Take me to a table with three robots, require you to purchase BBO non-refundable dollars.

**1** Select Help me find a game (see page 65)

**2** The first few times, choose the entry Take me to an interesting table

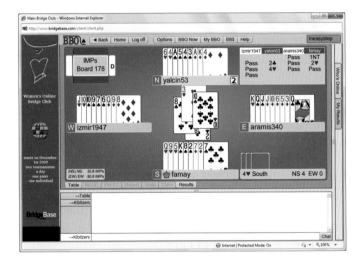

**3** When you want to leave the table, press Back

**4** Kibitz other games, or select one of the Play options, for example Take me to a table with three robots

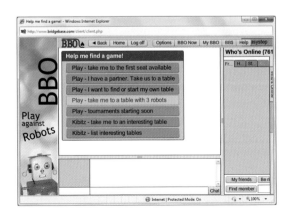

# 5 Internet Entertainment

*Use the Internet as your TV and Radio guide for regular channels or web broadcasts. Check what movies are being released, and what shows are on stage around the world. Or just relax to the sound of classical music.*

# What's on TV?

Every country has its national and regional television stations, along with numerous local stations. The Internet can help you keep track of them, and even look in on them, since many offer websites, and broadcast over the Internet.

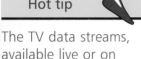
The TV data streams, available live or on demand from the websites, require bandwidth from 28.8 Kbps (dial-up rate) up to 2000 Kbps (broadband rate).

**1** Start with a visit to a TV Station directory, such as wwitv.com, which lists live and on-demand TV broadcasts from around the world

**2** Select a language and then a location, a region of the USA for example, to list all the TV stations available

The listing includes the web stream link, and a description of the type of content, for each of the TV stations in the specified location.

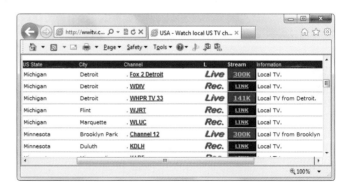

This displays a list of the prerecorded, video and live TV broadcasts available in the selected region.

3 Choose a live TV channel, for example WVVH, and click the button to view the channel content in your browser

4 Some live channels are restricted, e.g. BBC World News is excluded from the USA, UK and Japan. You will also find that some channels are chargeable and require a subscription

You need to subscribe to watch CNN International. Try it free for one week. Sign in if you're already a subscriber.

5 Streamed TV channels may use Windows Media Player (green links) or RealPlayer (blue links). The site will detect which player is needed and, if necessary, will prompt you to install or activate it

Download FREE RealPlayer SP

# Regular TV

Even if you want to watch regular TV (satellite, cable or antenna), the Internet proves useful for searching schedules.

**1** TV Zap has links to worldwide television schedules and guides, at the www.tvzap.com website

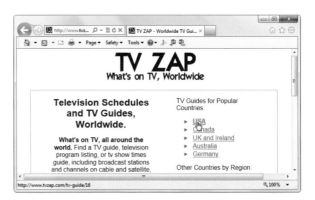

**Hot tip**

TV Zap offers a range of websites providing schedules and guides for the country, or region, you select, outlining the type of content so you can decide which will suit you best.

**2** Select your region or country, for example USA

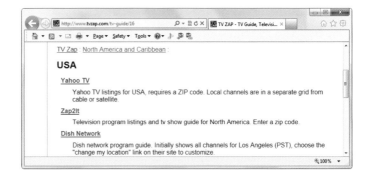

**Don't forget**

Along with the TV programme listings, you may find some special interest listings, such as the pick of this week's films on TV.

**3** Select one of the TV listings, e.g. Excite, then enter your zip code or your search criteria

# What's on Radio?

You can find out what's on terrestrial radio stations, and listen to radio stations that broadcast over the Internet.

**1** Type the web address radiostationworld.com in the browser address bar

## Hot tip

The original address for this website was TVRadioWorld.com, and this URL will still display the website. However, the emphasis has now switched to radio broadcasts.

**2** Click the Navigate link and search for radio stations, click the down-arrow to choose the location from the list for the selected region, and then click Go

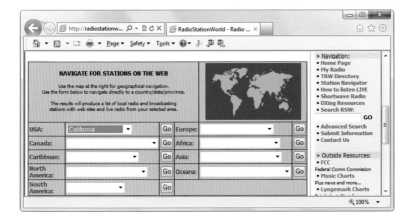

## Don't forget

As with TV over the Internet (see pages 68-9), you'll need a player to listen to the broadcast programs.

# Internet Radio

1 Review the region of interest, to see which locations have radio stations that may be of interest

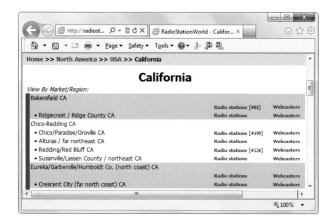

2 Choose a particular town or district from the list, for example San Jose/Santa Cruz (South Bay area)

3 Choose a radio station of interest in the selected area, for example KFFG in Los Altos

④ Each station has its transmission power, location, language and type of content identified

⑤ Click the speaker symbol for the radio station, to select it and listen live

⑥ You will be transferred to a window that identifies the media player required to play the radio stream

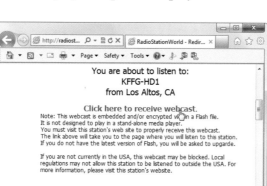

⑦ Click the link to receive the webcast. The required media player will be installed, or initialized, and the radio station should begin playing

⑧ Visit the radio station website for details of current or recently-played tracks, or to download any special software required

# Visit CBS TV

**1** Visit the CBS TV Network website at www.cbs.com

**2** Select Full Schedule for news of what's coming up

**3** Select Watch and choose the show you want to see

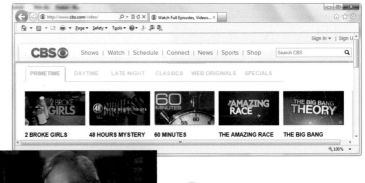

**4** Click an episode to view. The usual video controls are available

# NBC Services

You'll find similar facilities at the NBC website.

**1** Go to the website www.nbc.com and click Schedule

### Don't forget

You need to connect from a computer within the region, to be able to view the shows and take full advantage of the features offered.

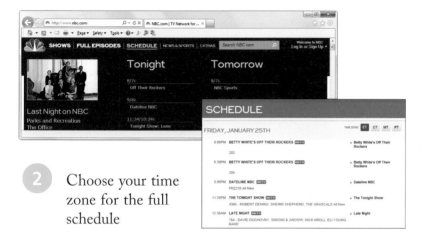

The video you have requested is not available for your geographic region.

**2** Choose your time zone for the full schedule

**3** Click Full Episodes to display a list of shows

### Hot tip

Click Shows and select a particular show for news, reviews, bios, episode guides, photos and related products.

**4** Choose a show, e.g. Days of our Lives, to list all the clips and episodes available

# The BBC Website

**1** Go to the BBC website at www.bbc.co.uk/ to view the appropriate version, National or International, of the home web page

**2** Scroll down to see the schedules for all the TV and radio channels

**3** Select a TV channel or radio station and click to listen

**4** Register at the BBC and you can add programs and clips to your Favorites to listen to later

# The Movies

Maybe movies are your preference. As you'd expect, the Internet has lots to say about them. For many people, the home of movies is in Hollywood, California.

**1** You'll find a comprehensive list of Hollywood movies at the www.hollywood.com website

**2** Select the Movies tab, and scroll down to the Directory for an alphabetical list of more than 280,000 movies, by title or celebrity

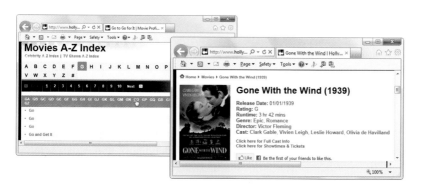

**3** Locate the movie title of interest and click for a synopsis and other details

## Hot tip

For UK films, visit the movie website at britishcinemagreats.com

## Don't forget

As usual, you can right-click the link and select Open Link in New Tab, rather than a separate window.

## Hot tip

If your interest is in Indian and Asian movies, visit the alternative movie website at www.bollywoodworld.com

# New York Theatre

If all the world's a stage for you, visit the theater websites to see what shows are on.

1   For New York City theater information, including show listings, look at www.newyorkcitytheatre.com/

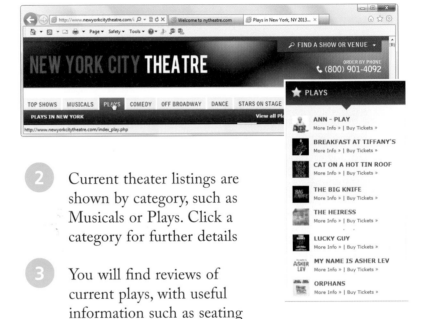

2   Current theater listings are shown by category, such as Musicals or Plays. Click a category for further details

3   You will find reviews of current plays, with useful information such as seating plans, run time, preview and final performance dates

4   Choose your date in the calendar for a list of all shows, the venue and ticket availability

**5** Use Google to find a New York theater district map

**6** Select the web page from Must See New York

**7** Click Theatre List to see all the theatres on the map, and move the mouse pointer over a name to locate it

**8** Click the theater name or the associated marker to display an information window with phone number, address and directions

# London Theatre Guide

**1** The www.officiallondontheatre.co.uk website has theater news, show lists, ticket purchase, awards etc.

**2** Click Select London Shows and use the filter to refine the list by date, location and genre

**3** The tab Plan Your Visit provides information and advice on the best and safest way to purchase tickets

**4** It also has travel tips and useful links to interactive maps and travel planners

# Classical Music Archives

If you'd simply like to relax to the sound of classical music, the Internet will not disappoint you.

**1** Visit www.classical-music-online.net to find a music collection that you can listen to – without charge

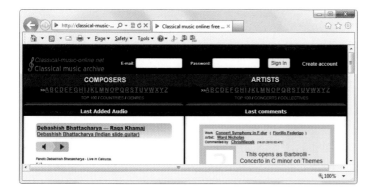

**Hot tip**

Members, registered free, can add comments and ask questions. You only need to supply an email address and nickname. The email address is never displayed.

**2** Select either Composer or Artist from the alphabetical links. Click E, for example, to link to a list of 57 composers. The number of recordings for each composer is indicated

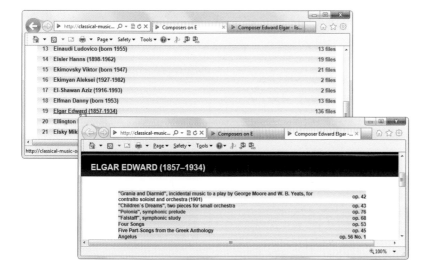

**Hot tip**

The chosen composer link opens in a new tab. The tabs have the same color to indicated that they are associated.

**3** Click your chosen composer to view the list of recordings offered

81

## ...cont'd

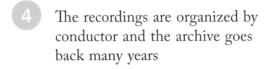

**4** The recordings are organized by conductor and the archive goes back many years

**5** When you select a particular recording, the length is indicated. You can listen online, or download

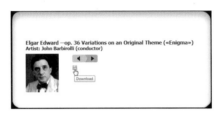

**6** The listed files cover a wide range of composers, including names such as Duke Ellington and Vangelis, not just the traditional classical names

**7** The site also offers a selection of videos. These are often recorded in the language native to the recording

**8** Scroll down the main page and beneath the Last Added video files, select View All

**9** Click a video to load it. On-screen controls allow you to choose the quality - 360 or 240, to watch full screen, pause and mute. The length of the video is also indicated

# 6 Arts and Crafts

*Whether you want to view pictures and drawings by contemporary artists or by old masters, or get help and advice for creating your own works of art, the Internet has information, and a host of tutorials, to help you improve your skills.*

# Web Gallery of Art

The Web Gallery of Art is a virtual museum, and searchable database, of European painting and sculpture:

**1** Go to the website www.wga.hu and click Enter Here

**2** Type the artist and the title (e.g. Vermeer, Girl with Pearl Earring) and the date or format, if known, then press Search to find matching pictures

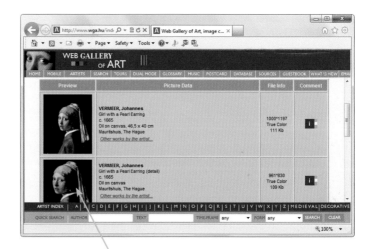

**3** Click the preview image to see the picture, or detail, full size. Click the Info button for comments and reviews

# Visit the Sistine Chapel

To see the features of the Web Gallery of Art in action, it is useful to take one of the predefined guided tours.

1   Click the Tours button and select the tour you wish to take, for example a visit to the Sistine Chapel in the Vatican

2   Click Start, then select a section of the tour to see detailed images and instructive comments

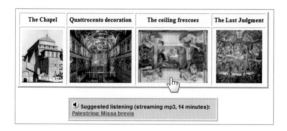

3   Some sections may be further subdivided, so you can explore in greater detail. For example, you can zoom in to view the Sistine Chapel ceiling close up

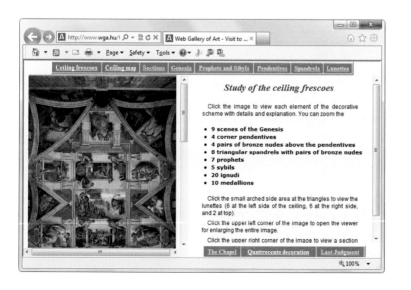

## Don't forget

There are 16 different guided tours defined on the website.

## Hot tip

Appropriate music to accompany the tour is suggested, in the form of a streaming MP3 that runs through Windows Media Player.

85

## Hot tip

This tour shows how you can click parts of the image to zoom in and see details and explanations. Other tours demonstrate more facilities, such as dual mode (side by side) presentations.

# Watercolor Painting

If you are interested in learning to paint in watercolor, or want to develop your skill, there are websites to help you.

**1** At www.watercolorpainting.com there are tutorials, step by step guides and lots of art-related links

**2** Click the Tutorials tab for an introduction to water color painting, and for basic or advanced tutorials

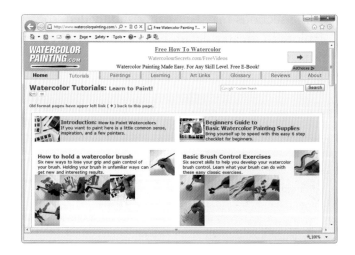

**3** Click Paintings for step by step painting guides, explaining the materials and techniques used

# Learn to Draw

Perhaps you've always wanted to draw, but never had the time. Now may be just the time to begin.

**1** Search for the phrase, learn to draw, for a list of websites related to this topic

**2** Select www.learn-to-draw.com, to get sets of easy to follow instructions for a variety of drawing tasks

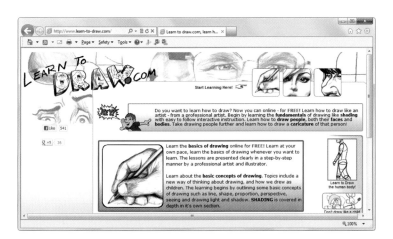

**3** Pick the tutorial that suits your existing skill level or interest and take advantage of the extra in-built links that explain terms and techniques

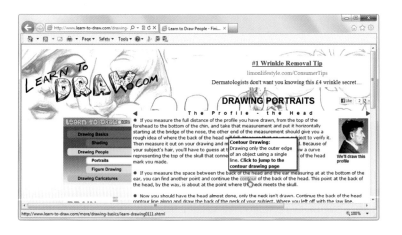

**Don't forget**

There will certainly be many websites offered. Some are purely for profit, some are there just to share an interest, while others turn out to be a mixture of both.

**Beware**

The instructions are free, but then you can donate to the site, which is supported by a large number of advertisements.

**Hot tip**

The page numbers at the bottom of each page indicate the page topic for ease of navigation.

# Video Art Lessons

There's video art tutorials available on the Virtual Instructor website.

 Visit http://thevirtualinstructor.com/ to access art lessons, instructions and videos of art techniques

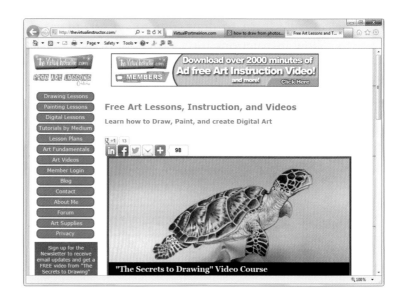

2 Select Tutorials by Medium, for example, for video instruction on pastels, charcoal, oils etc

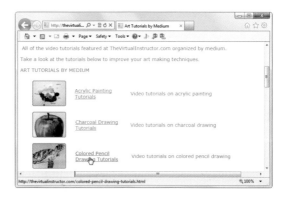

3 Some videos are excerpts of actual lessons, others are complete tutorials on how to draw a specific object

# Origami

What will you do with all that paper from your painting and drawing practice? Origami, the art of paper folding, sounds like the natural thing to try next.

**1** Go to www.scarygami.net/basic_folds.php to see the basic folds and to learn Origami terms

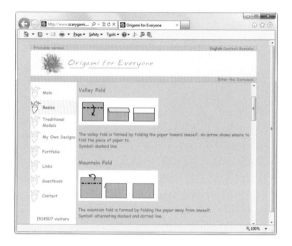

**Hot tip**

The Google search results may include images, such as Origami diagrams, as well as relevant web pages (1 million in this example).

**2** The Origami Basics section also explains base figures, the starting point for many models, and there are some diagrams for traditional models such as the Crane bird

The Traditional Crane

**3** Just type videos of origami into your search engine to see a wide range of origami projects created as you watch, via YouTube and other video providers

Videos of **origami**
bing.com/videos

6:42 · Origami Fireworks (Yami Yamauchi) · YouTube
8:48 · Origami Magic Ball · YouTube
Origami Rabbit (Hsi-Min Tai) · YouTube
3:04 · origami beating heart · YouTube

**Beware**

Many of the videos run without a problem. Some may redirect you to a site which encourages membership, and some will not play in all locations (countries).

**4** The length of the video is indicated and the usual controls, pause and volume control, are available

# Celtic Knots

Celtic knots are motifs created by loops or continuous threads. They can be found on ancient stonework and in illuminated manuscripts, and in the form of jewelry and tattoos. You can also design and draw them on paper.

**1** Go to www.aon-celtic.com, click the Knotwork link, then click the Basic Celtic Knotwork tutorial

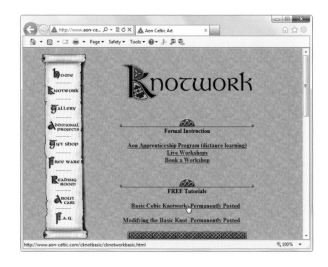

**2** Follow the steps in the tutorial to mark up a piece of graph paper, joining the sections and the corners, then deleting lines where threads overlap

## Beware

Associations, such as Love, Loyalty or Friendship, assigned to Celtic knot designs are inventions. The spiritual meanings of ancient symbols have been lost, while more recent symbols are merely decorative.

## Don't forget

This website adds a new tutorial each month, covering different types of Celtic knots, to encourage repeat visits.

## ...cont'd

You can draw Celtic knots in your browser, with the help of applications provided on the Internet.

**3** Go to www.bit-101.com/celticknots and click Draw to generate the Celtic knot, as defined by the settings

**4** Click on the cross-overs, or adjacent segments, to change the ways they are connected

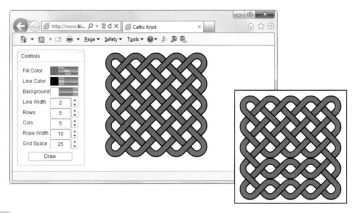

**5** Visit www.stevenabbott.co.uk/Knots/knots.html where you can download software to generate your own Celtic knot patterns

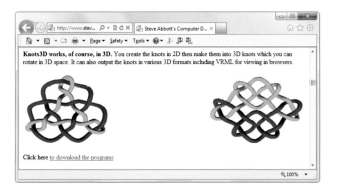

**6** Download the program, which should run under Windows Vista and later versions, to create knots in 2D and turn them into 3D which you can rotate in space

**Don't forget**

Drag the color sliders to change settings for Fill, Line and Background colors.

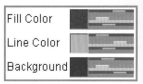

You can also set line width, number of rows and columns, rope width and grid space.

**Beware**

You must put a capital K in /Knots/ in this website address.

**Don't forget**

The website is created and managed by an individual for his own interest and is 'neither professional nor bombproof'! It does, however, provide an interesting insight into Celtic knot creation.

# Cross Stitch

If your preference is for textiles and threads, you can find tutorials and patterns galore. These are often free of charge, even on websites that are online shops.

Free cross stitch pattern
Hummingbird in Flight

Eastern Tiger Swallowtail Butterfly
Free Cross Stitch Pattern
If you are new to cross-stitch, you can learn from the Counted Cross Stitch Tutorial

Texas bluebonnet cross stitch pattern

1 Visit the site www. birdcrossstitch.com to display the free cross stitch patterns offered

2 Click on the image to display links for the pattern sheets

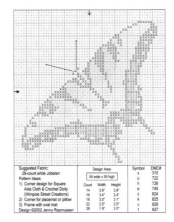

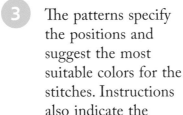

3 The patterns specify the positions and suggest the most suitable colors for the stitches. Instructions also indicate the finished size, using varying thread counts

4 The site also offers links to other sites where you will find a variety of free patterns

Eastern Tiger Swallowtail Butterfly

When planning a butterfly garden, remember to use larval food plants. In Central Texas, an important larval food for the Eastern Tiger Swallowtail is the Mexican plum, which also provides nectar for butterflies and food for birds.

Bird Cross Stitch Designs by Jenny Rasmussen. Visit Jenny on the web at www.BirdCrossStitch.com

If you are new to cross stitch, a tutorial will help. Many cross stitch websites reference the very comprehensive tutorial written by Kathleen Dyer. To view a copy:

**1** Go to home.comcast.net/~kathydyer/index.html and click the Counted Cross Stitch Tutorial link

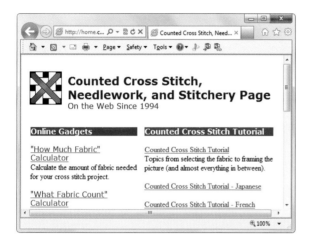

**2** At http://crossstitch.about.com there's a series of lessons and a list of free cross stitch patterns

**3** On the Basics tab you will find a video demonstration of how to do cross stitch

93

# Knitting

If you enjoy knitting and like to make items for charitable causes, you'll find inspiration at websites like Knitting Patterns Central at www.knittingpatternscentral.com

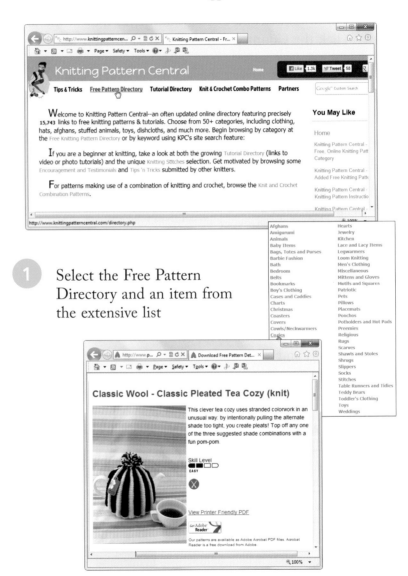

**1** Select the Free Pattern Directory and an item from the extensive list

**2** Choose an item for details of materials, instructions for knitting and finishing, and permission to use the pattern for personal or charity purposes only

# Guilds and Associations

Guilds and associations help you contact like-minded people, over the Internet or in local meetings.

**1** Visit the Knitting Guild Association (TKGA) website at www.tkga.com and click Guilds/Clubs

**Don't forget**

You'll find similar national associations for other countries, and for most crafts and hobbies.

**2** Select Find a Local Guild/Club and specify your city or state (e.g. Kansas) to obtain a list for your area

**3** Guilds are listed alphabetically. For a faster search press the Alt keyboard key to reveal the Menu bar

**Hot tip**

If there is no local group in your area, the association will advise and assist you in setting up your own local group.

**4** Click Edit, Find on this page, and type the state or town name into the Find field and press Enter

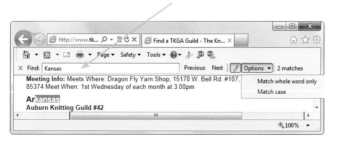

**Hot tip**

Use the Find options to navigate through the matches and the filter to narrow the search.

# Other Crafts

## Don't forget

About.com is now owned by the New York Times Company, so you'll find sponsored links and offers of supplies and equipment, but there will also be plenty of free information.

## Hot tip

The About.com guide for your selected topic will offer tutorials or projects, regular articles, and perhaps a newsletter, plus links to related websites.

If we haven't covered your favorite craft, search on Google, or explore a website, such as www.about.com, that provides preselected links for particular subjects.

1 Select a category such as Hobbies & Games, or alternatively use the alphabetical list at the foot of the web page

2 Alternatively, the website http://interweave.com covers many textile and other handicrafts

# 7 Travel Plans

The Internet provides you with the tools available to travel agents, so you can search for suitable deals, compare prices offered by different services, and create your own custom holiday. The Internet tells you what's going on at your chosen destination, and gives you maps to help you find your way there.

# World Wide Travel

There's a whole wide world of travel options available to you when you start planning a trip. You could be seeking a low cost holiday, or have a luxury holiday in mind. You might have plenty of time for research, or it could be a last-minute trip. Safety and comfort could be your key consideration, or you might be seeking adventure.

**Don't forget**

People over 50 make up the majority of travelers worldwide. They have the time and the freedom to travel, and, with the help of the Internet, can find options to match their interests and budgets.

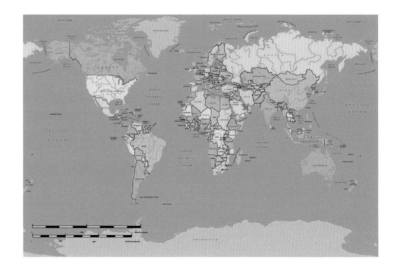

**Hot tip**

Which are the best websites for travel? Each will have its own particular strengths, so it all depends on what aspects you consider are important, how much of the work you are ready and able to do for yourself, and what time you have available for planning.

Whatever your requirements, the World Wide Web can help. There are many websites on the Internet devoted to one or more of the various aspects of travel, including:

- **Transportation** – air, sea, rail, road and river

- **Accommodation** – hotel, motel, b&b, self catering apartment, recreational vehicle, tent, camp site

- **Destinations** – domestic, overseas, remote location, single center, multicenter, tour, cruise

- **Activities** – sun and sand, sight seeing, city break, educational, cultural, sport, adventure, volunteer

- **Information** – maps, directions, guides, reviews, travel books, Internet access

- **Facilities** – itineraries, luggage, disabled suitability, currency, passports, adapters

# Online Travel Agents

The most natural choice, when you first start planning holidays on the Internet, is to use the online equivalent of the high street travel agent. There are a number of such websites, but Expedia is a popular choice.

**1** Go to www.expedia.com (or the version for your location) to research, plan and purchase your trip

**2** Click Sign in and then Create account. Fill in your first name and surname exactly as they appear on your passport, your email address and password

**3** Accept the terms and conditions then click Create Expedia Account

**4** If you prefer not to create an account, you can explore the website as a guest, or search for your itinerary

### Beware

You can only purchase tickets and holidays from the version of the website meant for your home location, i.e. www.expedia.

| | |
|---|---|
| com | USA |
| au | Australia |
| ca | Canada |
| fr | France |
| de | Germany |
| it | Italy |
| nl | Netherlands |
| co.uk | UK |

**99**

### Hot tip

If you choose to create an account, you will find certain advantages, such as being able to save itineraries, earn discount vouchers and specify and save preferences.

# Book Flights

Most travel plans start with the flights, since these are often the limiting factor, due to their cost or the availability of seats.

## Don't forget

Click the date box to display a calendar, and select the desired date. Specify My dates are flexible if appropriate.

**1** At www.expedia.com, select Flight only, and then enter the Departing From city and Going To city

**2** Set the departing and returning dates and times, and select the number and type of passengers

**3** Click Search for Flights to look for round trips between the selected cities, on the specified dates and times

## Don't forget

Start to type in the Leaving from box, and select from the drop-down list of airports.

**4** Refine the search by specifying particular airlines, departure times or choose direct or refundable flights

## ...cont'd

For example, you could select New York (JFK) and Vancouver (YVR), and request direct flights to produce a shortlist of options:

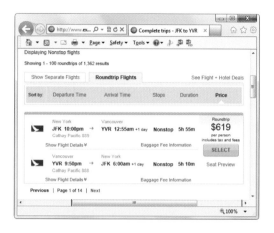

1. Review the flights offered, then click Select for the trip that you want

2. Check the rules and restrictions that apply, e.g. This fare is nonrefundable

3. You may be offered the chance to add a hotel or a rental car to your booking

4. Select to continue with the booking and provide payment details

5. Alternatively, choose Save this itinerary, or click Cancel and go to the home page, to discard the suggestions

**Important Flight Information**

We want you to know the airline you're traveling with has the following restrictions regarding your flight.

- Tickets are **nonrefundable** and **nontransferable**. A fee of $100 per ticket is charged for itinerary changes. Name changes are not allowed.

- The airline may charge additional fees for checked baggage or other optional services.

**Don't forget**

You can View flights separately, to select the departure flight and the return flight individually, or View complete round-trips.

**Hot tip**

The tickets are not purchased, and the fares are not guaranteed, until you have supplied your credit card details and confirmed the order.

# Book your Hotel

You can choose to book your hotel rooms while you are purchasing your flight tickets, or you can treat this as a separate transaction.

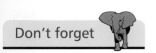
## Don't forget

You may make additional savings if you purchase flights, and book your hotel or rental car, in the same transaction, but you'll have less flexibility.

**1** At www.expedia.com, select Hotel only, then enter the Destination city or airport, e.g. Vancouver

**2** Set the check-in and the check-out dates, then select the number of rooms, and the number of adults and children

## Hot tip

Use the filter to specify the hotel name, star rating or average price.

**3** Click Search for hotels to list the hotels near your destination

## Don't forget

Click a selected hotel for a Quick View which gives details of facilities and a location map.

**4** You can specify preferences to limit the list, and you can also see the hotels on a map

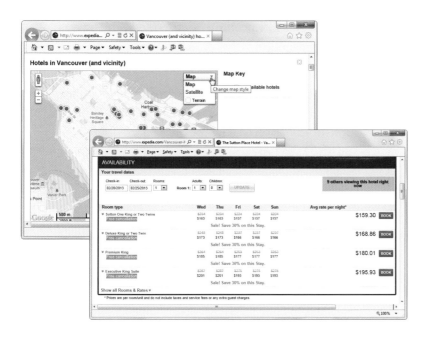

### Hot tip

Expedia uses Google maps. You can zoom in and pan to the area that interests you, and use the Pegman icon for a street view (see page 111).

**5** Use the images, the hotel amenities and guest reviews to help select a hotel and then click to book

## Booking Direct

If you regularly stay with a particular chain of hotels, you may prefer to book direct. For example, to choose a hotel from the Intercontinental chain (Holiday Inn etc.), go to www.ichotelsgroup.com and specify your requirements.

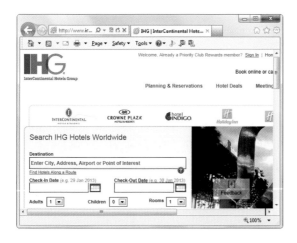

### Hot tip

You might choose to book directly with Intercontinental, if you join their Priority Club Rewards scheme (see page 106). Other hotels have similar schemes.

# Book a Rental Car

You can book a rental car along with your flight tickets, or in a separate transaction.

**Hot tip**

Use the Filter By: Unlimited mileage to refine the results.

**1** At www.expedia. com, select Car only, then the Pick-up location and the Car type

**2** Choose the pick-up and the drop-off dates and times, and click the Search for Cars button

The cars are displayed in price bands, but you can display them by car size or car hire company.

**Hot tip**

Expedia indicates the location of the rental car desk, and if a shuttle bus is required.

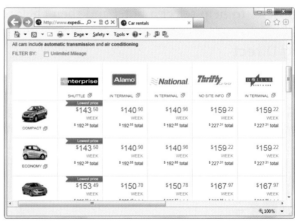

**Don't forget**

You can also book directly with the car rental company. This may give you better pick-up and drop-off options.

**3** Scroll to find your preferred car size and click to see the full details for a particular car. Charges are shown in your home currency

**4** Continue the booking to confirm the driver details and book the car, or save the details in your itinerary

# Other Online Travel Agents

If you have the time, run the same travel query on several of the travel agency websites and explore the differences.

Like Expedia, the www.travelocity.com website helps you book flights, hotels, cars, holidays and cruises. When you go to the website it recognizes your location and offers the appropriate booking site.

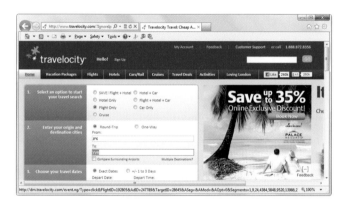

Orbitz at www.orbitz.com, set up by a group of American airlines but now independently owned, offers similar services.

If you are in Europe, visit Opodo at www.opodo.com and select the country you are in, to try more local-based options and perhaps with better local knowledge.

## Hot tip

Websites, such as the travel companies, will often remember details of your searches, even if you give them no personal details, such as name and email address. The website will use a 'cookie' to enable it to remember the activity that took place when you visited their website. This means that next time you visit you will see the result of previous searches, or information that the website thinks might be of interest.

105

# Loyalty Cards

## Beware

Keep track of the members of an alliance, since they may change.

Airlines operate programs to encourage travelers to stay loyal to the particular airline, or alliance of airlines. For example, American Airlines operates its own AAdvantage program and participates in the OneWorld program, with British Airways, Cathay Pacific, Qantas and other airlines.

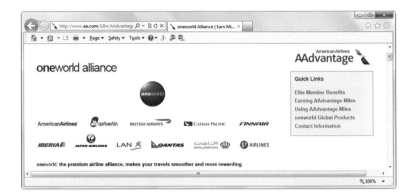

## Don't forget

Some online booking options may exclude loyalty cards and points, or may offer their own alternatives, such as Nectar points at Expedia, so take this into account when choosing an option.

Hotels also offer loyalty programs, which earn miles (in collaboration with airline programs) or points, that can be exchanged for accommodation or other goods and services.

## Hot tip

All loyalty programs include elite levels, such as silver or gold, awarded when you attain a certain number of air miles or points during the membership year.

Car rental companies also offer loyalty programs, which can be linked to various hotel and airline loyalty programs.

Hertz Gold Plus Rewards
Login   Join Now

# Last-Minute Bookings

Last-minute booking is perhaps the complete antithesis of loyalty programs – you have to take whatever you can get.

**1**   Visit website www.priceline.com, and enter your journey details for a round-trip or one way journey

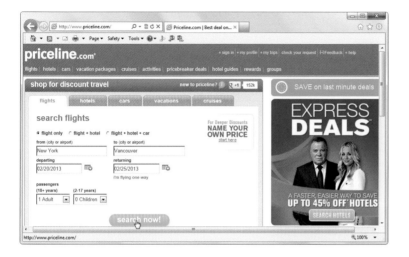

**2**   Click Search Now to list flights available from a variety of airlines

**3**   Choose your preferred option from the lowest price flights or the non-stop flights

# Name your Own Price

## Don't forget

Since you provide the price, not the supplier, this is known as a reverse auction.

With Priceline, you can make a bid for a flight, with your requirements and the price you are willing to pay, and see if any supplier is willing to accept it.

1   Search flights at www.priceline.com, and select Start Here to name your own price

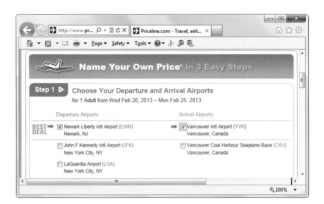

## Hot tip

The price you specified will be adjusted by Priceline to include fees.

2   Confirm the departure and arrival airports to be used

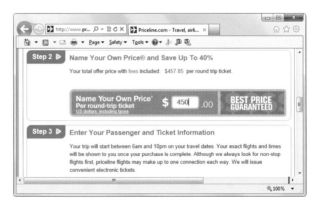

## Beware

If an airline accepts your price, tickets will be purchased. These will be non-refundable, non-transferable and non-changeable. They are not eligible for frequent flyer miles.

3   Specify your total offer and enter your name, date of birth and gender. You are able to preview the details before you enter credit card information

4   Click Buy my tickets now and await a response to your request for the flight

# Travel Guide

To help you explore your destination and surroundings, you need a travel guide that will tell everything you need to know, laid out in a clear and consistent format.

**1** Go to www.roughguides.com and click the Find a destination tab for an alphabetical list of countries

**2** Where a country is covered, the guide gives advice on items such as When to go, Where to go and Essentials, as well as details of hotels, attractions, restaurants and things to do

**3** The Lonely Planet Guide at www.lonelyplanet.com has a similar approach with tips and articles on hundreds of destinations

**4** Also look at tripadvisor.com, for reviews from fellow travelers, citing their experiences, good and bad

**Hot tip**

Rough Guides is a publisher of travel and reference material. Destinations marked with a map pin symbol include more detailed information.

109

**Don't forget**

Most of these websites are inherently commercial and want to sell you trips and literature.

# Google Maps

**Hot tip**

You can start off at any Google site, as long as you include the country in your map search.

For an alternative map of your destination and surroundings:

**1** Open the Google website and select Maps

**2** Enter the place you are seeking, for example Christchurch, New Zealand, and click the Search button, or select the correct name if it is suggested

**3** Use the zoom controls to enlarge the area of the map you wish to view in detail

**4** Click the Satellite button to get a bird's eye view

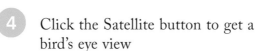

**Hot tip**

Optimize the area of the map visible by hiding the Information panel and reinstating it when required.

**5** Click the symbol to hide the Information panel. The symbol changes to the show the panel symbol

**6** Click and drag the Pegman icon onto the street map to get a street view of the location

**Don't forget**

You can sign in to Google to save or share places that are important to you.

**7** Drag the picture to move along, or re-orientate the view (360° horizontally, 270° vertically). You can also use the Pegman in the bottom corner of the window to quickly reposition or reorientate yourself

**Don't forget**

Streets for which there are street views, are outlined in blue.

**8** Use the inbuilt Link tool to email the specific location to your contacts

**9** Click the printer icon to view a printable map. Zoom in to the location and to get the degree of detail that is required. Click Print when ready

111

# Plan a Road Trip

If you are planning a driving holiday, it's useful to have printed directions, with distances, timings and road numbers. For a dedicated route planner.

 Visit www.randmcnally.com for trips around Canada and the USA and click Maps and Directions

## Don't forget

Multimap was acquired by Microsoft and merged into Bing maps in 2007. Bing maps are very similar to Google maps, providing similar functions, but not as comprehensive.

For most regions of the world you can use the maps included in Google

Click Maps and enter the starting address, city/town or post code, click Find or select from the suggested locations

## Don't forget

With a Google ID, you can sign in and save the planned route to My Maps.

**4** Click Get directions and add the destination details, again selecting from the suggested list if necessary

**5** Click the arrows to reverse the direction of travel

**6** Select Add destination to include more stopping points or to extend the journey. You are able to add numerous points on the itinerary

**7** Click Get directions for a full, itemized route with estimated travel time, road numbers and distances between junctions indicated

**8** Select any individual point on the route for specific instructions with the option of viewing the street view of the intersection

**Hot tip**

Right-click your destination on the map for it to be automatically added into the Destination field.

**Hot tip**

Drag the blue route marker on the map at any point to change the route.

Change the order of the destinations by dragging the A, B, C, into a different sequence.

113

# Print Trip Guide

When you have completed and saved the route if required (see page 112), you can print the trip.

Print

Click the printer icon and choose Text only for a step by step list of the route

(see page 112)

## Hot tip

You also have the option to print a map of the route. You can print the full route, or zoom before printing to a particular area, such as a town or city.

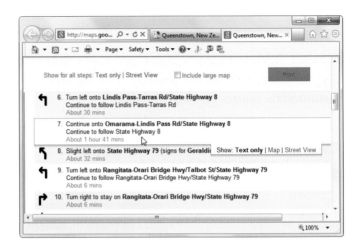

Any specific instruction can be illustrated in Map or Street View to help with navigation

Choose Street View for printing a picture of each intersection or road change

## Beware

If you choose to print the street view for a journey of some length, it could take much paper and ink.

# Traffic Reports

For a road trip, a key factor will be the traffic situation. There are numerous websites devoted to this, no matter where you are traveling. For the United States and Canada:

**1** Go to www.highwayconditions.com and select the state or province where you will be traveling

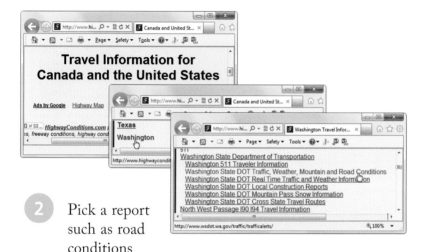

**2** Pick a report such as road conditions

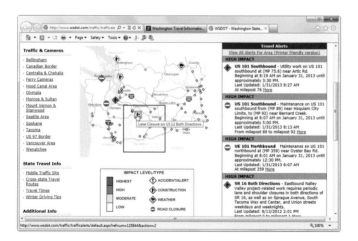

**3** Zoom to view more routes with problems reported

**4** Select a Traffic & Cameras area such as Seattle for the detailed traffic status

**Hot tip**

For the UK, Frixo.com gives live traffic news and information, with details of delays and incidents that may affect your journey.

**Don't forget**

This map identifies current incidents and classifies them according to type and level, so you can judge the likely effect on your journey.

# Weather Reports

Whatever method of travel you use for your journey, up-to-date information about the weather will be important. Again, the Internet is a ready source. For example:

**1** Go to www.weather.com and enter the zip, city or place for which you'd like a current weather report

**2** To change location click the button and select the relevant location

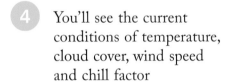

**3** Enter the city name, or select the required city from the list

**4** You'll see the current conditions of temperature, cloud cover, wind speed and chill factor

**5** There is the outlook for overnight and the next day. Click Full day forecast for more detail

**6** The site provides a 10-day forecast, monthly and seasonal prediction

**7** Use the facilities on the Map area to view Satellite (clouds), Radar (rain) and Aerial images

# (8) Explore your Family Tree

*The Internet has created a whole new way to search for information on your family background and your ancestors. You can share information with other parts of your family, without having to travel, even if your ancestral roots are from far distant shores.*

# Introduction to Genealogy

The term Genealogy applies to the study of the history of past and present members of a particular family. It also applies to the records and documentation that describe that history, the members of the family, and their relationships.

Genealogy is highly popular right across the world. There are many reasons why you might research your family's history:

- Simple curiosity about yourself and your roots

- Making your children aware of their ancestors

- Preserve family cultural and ethnic traditions

- Family medical history (inherited disease or attribute)

- Join a lineage or heritage society

Getting started is generally quite easy – you find the oldest living members of your family and ask them about other members, especially those who are no longer here to answer for themselves.

After the first flush of success, however, it could become difficult to fill in the gaps and extend the history further back in time. You have to rely on official records, and this could require a lot of travel, especially if your family originated overseas. Fortunately, much of the necessary legwork can now be accomplished over the Internet, there's plenty of advice and guidance, and you'll be able to capitalize on the research that others have carried out.

The information you glean can be recorded on charts designed to organize genealogical data.

- Ascendant, Ahnentafel and Pedigree charts

- Descendant, Progenitor charts

- Family Group sheets

These forms, and the way to use them, are described in various tutorials (see page 121).

# Researching your Family Tree

If you are new to genealogy, perhaps the best place to start is with an online (and free) genealogy tutorial.

**1** There's a tutorial on Researching Your Family Tree at www.learnwebskills.com/family/intro.html which provides a self-paced introduction

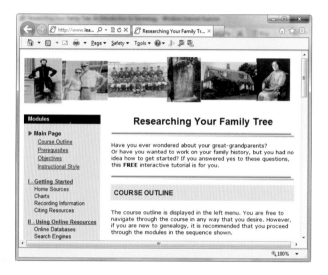

**2** Follow the modules in this tutorial to research your own ancestors while learning to use the genealogical charts, online databases and other resources

**3** The site gives advice on how you can get help with your research by contact with other researchers. It provides links to RootsWeb's Discussion Lists and Message Boards where you can share ideas and issues with others

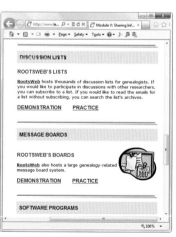

## Hot tip

Search Google for "Genealogy Tutorial" (the quotes mean the exact phrase), and you get 8,400 matching web pages.

## Hot tip

The navigation bar on the left lists the contents of the six modules, plus more than 10 useful website links.

## Don't forget

The Tools section of the navigation bar has links to charts (see page 121).

# About Genealogy

**Don't forget**

Although this website is supported from the USA, the class is geared to genealogy researchers in all countries.

1. For a somewhat more structured introduction, go to genealogy.about.com and scroll to the Topics section

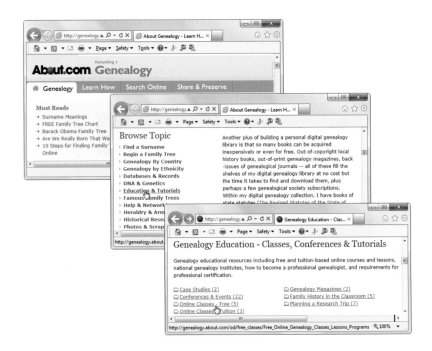

**Hot tip**

Enter your email address and click Sign Up to subscribe to the About Genealogy newsletter.

2. Select Education & Tutorials and scroll down to Online Classes – Free

This class consists of four lessons:

- Genealogical Basics
- Family & Home Sources
- Genealogy Research 101
- Vital Records – Birth, Marriage, Death, Divorce

The genealogy.about.com site has a variety of tools to help you organize your research and keep track of your discoveries.

**1** Click the Learn How tab and scroll down to Organize and Record Your Research

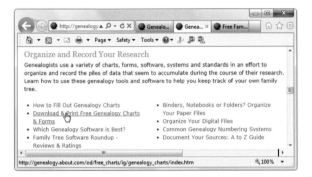

**2** Click the link to open a window displaying three typical, interactive, family tree and pedigree charts

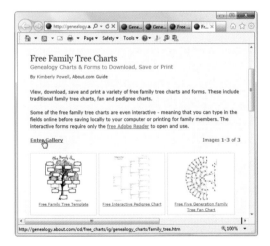

**Hot tip**

Right click the links on this website and choose Open in new tab. It's then easier to navigate the site and switch from page to page.

**Don't forget**

You will need Acrobat Reader 5.5 or later to be able to use the form.

**3** Click Enter Gallery and scroll down to find the Download link. The charts can be completed on the computer and saved or printed

# Genealogy Charts

**1** Go to the website www.mymclp.org and click the Genealogy link

**2** Scroll to the Family History Forms and select Six Generation Chart

### Don't forget

Right-click the link and select Save target as, to save a copy of the PDF file onto your hard drive (or click the Diskette icon in the browser view).

**3** The form opens as a .pdf document where you can begin to add information

**4** Save, print or email the form, or convert to Word

### Hot tip

Use the Zoom controls to make adding your details easier.

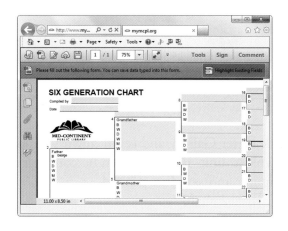

# Vital Records

When you've collected all the information you can from family members, and organized it using genealogy charts, you'll have a list of unanswered questions, and you'll need to start searching records to find some of the answers.

There are two main types of genealogical records that you can investigate:

## Original records

An original record is an account of a specific event, written at or near the time the event took place. Historically, many civil and religious authorities kept records on events in the lives of people in their jurisdictions. Original records include:

- **Vital Records** (birth, marriage, divorce and death)

- **Church Records** (christenings, baptisms, confirmations, marriages, or burials)

- **Cemetery Records** (names, dates and relationships)

- **Census Records** (household member name, sex, age, country or state of birth, occupation)

- **Military, Probate, Immigration Records**

## Compiled records

A compiled record is a collection of information on a specific person, family group or topic. Compiled records exist because others have already researched original records, or collated information from other compiled records, or other sources. Compiled records include:

- **Ancestral File** (over 35 million names, linked into ancestors and descendants)

- **International Genealogical Index** (computerized index of about 250 million names extracted from birth, christening, marriage, and other records)

- **Published Family Histories, Biographies, Genealogies, and Local Histories**

Hot tip

You may be able to access original records on microfiche, and some, especially census records, have been indexed and computerized.

Don't forget

Compiled records are useful if you want to learn about ancestors who were born before 1900, but are not likely to have information about modern families.

Hot tip

The two main compiled record files were developed by the family history department of the Church of Latter-Day Saints (see page 125).

# Cyndi's List

To find out where to look for original records, you should start at www.cyndislist.com, a search engine that is dedicated to genealogical research via the Internet. You can search for helpful websites by location, or by record type.

**1** Click Categories and B, Beginners, and you'll be able to view lists of websites related to researching various types of original and vital records

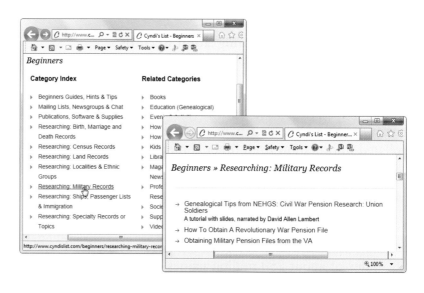

**2** Researching Military Records, for example, gives links to relevant help files and ideas of the next step

# FamilySearch

The www.familysearch.org website, owned and operated by the Church of Latter-day Saints, provides free family history.

**1** Complete the form with as much information as you can. The minimum you need to provide is the surname. Tick the box Match exactly if you are certain of the spelling

**2** Select Search with a life event for which you have more details, such as date of marriage

**3** The matching records are displayed for review. Click on the name to view the source of the information, which may come with a photograph of the actual written record

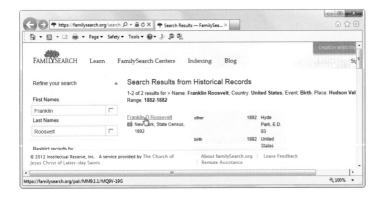

# Ancestry.com

You can search for ancestors at www.ancestry.com
This website has many databases, including census, birth, marriage, death, military and immigration. It offers paid membership subscriptions, but there is a free Registered Guest account, which allows you to receive free email tips and build an online family tree, with access to some of the databases.

**Don't forget**

If you are interested in Canadian data, evaluate Ancestry.ca instead. For United Kingdom data, try Ancestry.co.uk
You can sign on at either website using your Ancestry.com guest account.

**1** Register for a Guest account on the home page

**Hot tip**

The guest account allows you to explore the databases, on your 14 day free trial, until you have confirmed that there is useful data available.

**2** Complete the details to create the free 14 day trial account with name, email and password and click continue

**3** You will be sent a confirming email with your username and password

**Don't forget**

Make a note of your username and password for future access. On this occasion you are immediately signed in.

**4** Start by creating a simple Family Tree with the details you already have

# ...cont'd

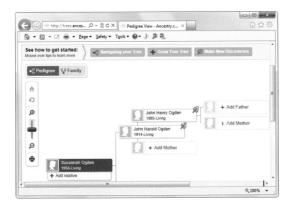

**Don't forget**

Most of the databases that appear on the Historical Records page are locked and only available to subscribers.

**5** As you fill in the information, small leaves may appear, indicating potential matches

**6** Click the hint to see the source of the information

**7** Click Search records on the person's name in the Family tree view to see potential matches

**8** To see full details, register and give a credit card number for a full membership account

**Beware**

For nearly all online sources of census information there is a charge. Even the British site National Archives at www.nationalarchives.gov.uk has commercial partners. These partners have enabled more information to be digitized, but at a cost to the researcher.

127

# US National Archives

More than 95 percent of the records in the National Archives are declassified and available for research purposes.

Some of the answers to your questions may be found in the US National Archives, at www.archives.gov

**Hot tip**

While you may not find the actual records online, you will find search aids online, such as microfilm indexes, and guidance on how to conduct research in the different types of records.

1 Select the Genealogists link, where you'll find help and guidance to get started

2 Select Tools for Genealogists, which includes links to free databases, help with using the Archival Research Catalog and links to other resources

**Hot tip**

There is unlimited access to Ancestry Library and Heritage Quest services, free-of-charge, from any NARA facility nationwide.

3 You can visit one of the National Archives centers in person for some of your research. The centers include National Archives, Federal Records and Presidential Libraries

# Other National Archives

Other countries will have their own national archives. For Australian information, go to www.naa.gov.au, then, under Using the Archives, click Family history.

You'd visit www.collectionscanada.ca for Canadian records, and select Genealogy and Family History.

The UK has its records at www.nationalarchives.gov.uk Select the Records tab to find guidance to available material.

**Hot tip**

Any person is entitled to visit the archives and use the services. It isn't necessary to be an Australian citizen or resident.

**Don't forget**

When you visit the Canadian website, you must select the English or French version.

**Hot tip**

There are around 300 in-depth guides on the UK National Archives website, to help you with your research.

# Immigrant Records

If parts of your family are from overseas, you will need to find the connection between the family groups. Immigration records may be the answer.

In the USA, the website www.immigrantships.net makes passenger lists available from a number of ships.

Ellis Island, just off Manhattan Island, New York, became the gateway to the United States from 1892 to 1924, for over 20 million immigrants. See website www.ellisisland.org

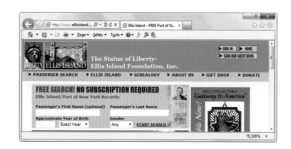

For information about UK immigration records, go to the website www.genealogy-guide.org.uk/immigration.html

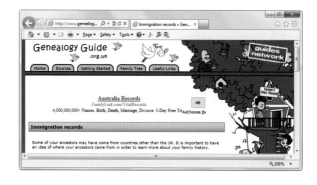

# 9 Digital Photography

*Find advice and guidance on the Internet to improve your skill. Store and back up your digital photographs, and print online photos. Share your photos with friends and family, and view the results from using various cameras and lenses.*

# Tips on the Internet

To help you get started, there are websites that tell you how to improve your digital photography skills and techniques.

1 Fuji has some tips for better photographs at the website www.everypicturematters.com
Select the Tips tab and scroll down to read the current tips

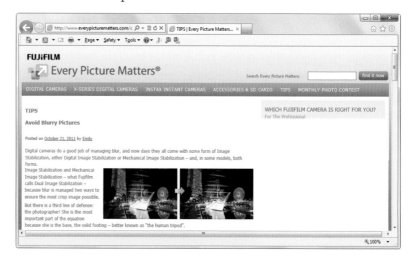

2 There's a more comprehensive website offered by Kodak. Go to www.kodak.com and select the button for Support and Downloads

3 Click the tab Tips and Projects Center. The Learn section shows ways to enhance and restore photos. The Create section has suggestions for home-made projects and there are tips from the experts

132

# Tutorials

There are numerous tutorials on various aspects of digital photography, some for beginners, for example those at the ShortCourses website:

**1** Switch to www.shortcourses.com/workflow for a short course on digital photography workflow

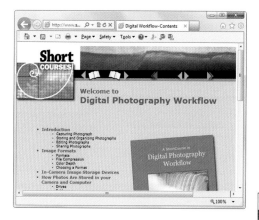

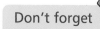

**2** Click the Home page link to see the full list of the short courses that are on offer. You can view them freely online, or download a PDF version (for a fee)

**3** If you are ready for a challenge, view the tutorial Making fine prints in your digital darkroom, at the www.normankoren.com website

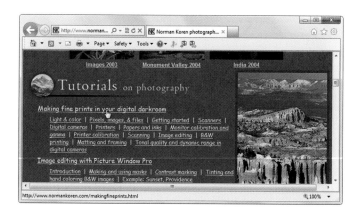

**Don't forget**

Click the Tutorials on Photography link (or add the #Tutorials bookmark to the website address) to display the list of tutorials.

**Hot tip**

This is a multi-part series that introduces tools and techniques for making fine prints digitally, to meet the highest aesthetic and technical standards.

# Find Inspiration

Digital photography is not just about equipment and techniques, it is also about subject and composition. Perhaps the best way to explore these aspects is through viewing the work of other photographers, for example at the Photographic Society of America.

**1** Visit www.psa-photo.org to see a series of examples. Click the Galleries link to select a gallery, and choose members by name to view their work

**2** View The Royal Photographic Society exhibitions at www.rps.org/
Click Exhibitions for more inspiration and the option to compete in a variety of categories

# Share Photos Online

You can use the Internet to share your digital photographs. You don't have to join a society and create a portfolio, and the photographs can be private, just for friends and family.

**1** Visit www.flickr.com and click Sign up

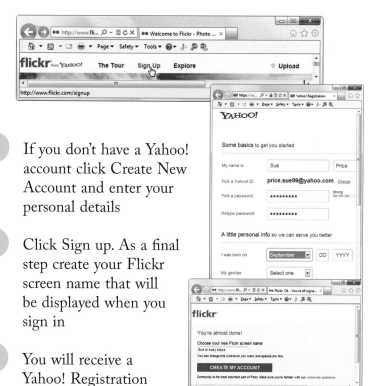

**2** If you don't have a Yahoo! account click Create New Account and enter your personal details

**3** Click Sign up. As a final step create your Flickr screen name that will be displayed when you sign in

**4** You will receive a Yahoo! Registration confirmation with your secret Sign in details and an email message to the same effect

**5** You can now begin to upload photos

135

### Hot tip

Flickr is a subsidiary company of Yahoo!. If you already have a Yahoo! ID you can use that to sign in.

### Don't forget

If you are located outside the US, click the link at the bottom of the page and select your country before registering, to get local prices and shipping charges.

# Upload Photographs

**1** Click Choose photos and videos to upload. You are advised of your photo and video storage limit

**2** Navigate through your picture folders to find the photos to share and click to select

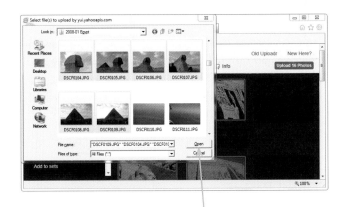

**3** Select photos and click Open to add them, then click Upload to transfer them

# View Albums

1. You will be informed if the upload is successful, and you are then able to start organizing and editing your photos

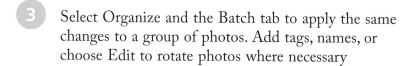

2. Click the details beneath an individual photo to change the name, add a description or comment or remove it from the Photostream

3. Select Organize and the Batch tab to apply the same changes to a group of photos. Add tags, names, or choose Edit to rotate photos where necessary

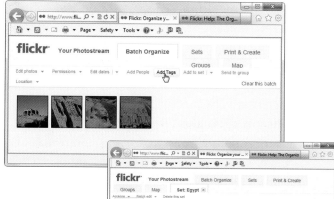

4. Create sets of photos, maybe of an event or holiday and view them separately

**Hot tip**

Click Location to add your batch of photos to a map of the world. Zoom right in to locate as near as possible the exact location.

**Beware**

Photos are automatically Public when uploaded. Change the Visibility before uploading or use the Batch option once uploaded to change Permissions to your preferred state.

**Don't forget**

Add more photos to a set, delete items, or search for other images to add to the set.

# Share Albums

Invite your friends and family to view your photographs:

Click Contacts and Import your Contacts, or alternatively Send Invites

**2** If your invitation is accepted and the contact opens a Flickr account, you can mark them as Family or Friend and they are able to view all your photos, public and private, and add comments

**3** Alternatively, for public photos, click Share this on the main Photostream page. Flickr offers a number of ways to share, including to generate an email sent through Flickr

**4** You can also Grab the link to the web address that you can paste into your own email message

You can share private photos even if your contact doesn't want a Flickr account with a Guest Pass.

5    Click Share this on the Photostream page and select email

6    Complete the details and tick the Family box. Flickr then changes the selection to include those images with the correct permissions

7    The email is sent with a Guest pass and the Family photos can be viewed

Similarly, your friends can invite you to share their albums, by sending you an email. To accept the invitation:

1    Click the link in your email, to view your friend's slideshow

2    You can treat the shared photos just like your own and share them with others

3    Click an individual photo to add tags or identify people

# Order Prints

Flickr provides a printing service which is part of their motivation for providing storage on the Internet. They use Snapfish, a division of Hewlett Packard. Flickr stores the original image file (even though slideshows use reduced images) so prints will be full quality.

 Sign in to your Flickr account, select Photostream and click Organize

**140**

2 Select the Print and Create tab to start selecting the relevant photos, then drag and drop them into the selection area

 Click Select all to add the photos at once or use the Search option to specify particular photos. Then click Order prints

4 Choose the print size and click Add to cart and then Proceed to Checkout

5 You will be transferred to Snapfish where you will need to register if this is your first visit

6 Snapfish completes your details for you – you just need to create a password. Accept the terms and conditions and click Continue

7 Your photographs are transferred to Snapfish where you are able to specify paper type, border and photo size

141

8 Make any necessary adjustments, and click Check out. Add a promotion code and delivery details or choose Pick up in store

9 Complete the payment process. You aren't committed until you Place the Order

# Storage Policy

**142**

To check the storage policy for your Flickr account:

1 Sign in to Flickr, select your account image (also known as your buddy image) and choose Settings

2 Your storage status is displayed as percentage used, which, with Flickr, is limited by monthly upload and currently two videos

3 Click upload capacity to learn more, and to read about ways in which you can reduce your requirement for online storage space

As you upload your images, you are told how much storage they will take. If you intend to print off the images using an online facility, you should maintain the resolution of the original picture

If, however, you intend the photos to be viewed just online, then you can reduce the resolution and therefore the storage space required.

4 Open the image in Windows Photo Gallery, right click the copy and choose Resize

# Other Online Photo Sites

There are other websites that offer free online photo storage, Shutterfly, for example, at www.shutterfly.com
The website offers a photo printing service and has connections with print specialists.

## Hot tip

Shutterfly has taken over the Kodak Gallery website which was previously Ofoto. Don't be surprised if web addresses change, but you will usually be redirected automatically.

Google's Picasa has storage facilities and online photo sharing. Register at picasaweb.google.com/
You can also download photo editing software at Picasa.

## Don't forget

Printing your photos at home using an inkjet or photo printer will give you instant results, but is unlikely to deliver quality comparable with a professional processor.

For simply getting prints of your photographs, in the most economical way, use a dedicated print service, such as those offered by for example Walmart at photo.walmart.com

In the UK you would choose a site such as www.truprint.co.uk

# PBase Galleries

The PBase photo sharing and hosting site encourages public viewing, giving serious photographers the opportunity to display their skills to the world. You'll usually find information on the settings and equipment used, and lots of comments made by other viewers.

**1** The PBase website is at www.pbase.com
Click Popular Galleries to view slideshows, or click the Search button to look for particular subjects

**2** For example, a search for Auroras produced several pages of fascinating Northern Lights slideshows

# 10 For the Grandchildren

Here we look at sharing your computer with the grandchildren when they come to visit. You can give them their own user identity, control their web activities, and encourage safe web browsing. We look at websites that will enable you to help and educate them, while also entertaining them.

# Create a User Account

To avoid problems that arise when you share your computer with others, especially children, give them their own User Account. Your own files and desktop settings will then remain secure, and cannot be affected or changed by their actions.

1. Go to Start, Control Panel and select Add or remove user accounts, in the User Accounts and Family Safety section

2. In the Manage Accounts window, select Create a new account

3. Choose Standard user, and click Create Account. The account will appear with an image automatically allocated

4. Double-click the new account and select Change the picture, to allow the child to select a personalized image

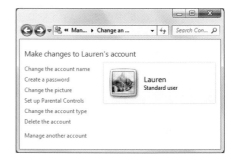

# Set Up Parental Controls

With the account now active, take the opportunity to manage which programs and games the child can access, and how much time can be spent on the computer.

1. In User Accounts and Family Safety, choose Set up parental controls for any user

2. Check that Additional controls are set to None and single click the child's account to view the Parental Controls included in Windows

3. Turn Parental Controls on. You will now be able to create time limits, and control access to games and other programs

**Hot tip**

You may be asked to sign in to Windows Live Family Safety if it has been installed. It offers a greater degree of safety and monitoring (see pages 148-9 for details).

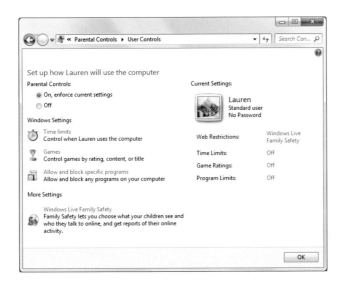

4. Choose Time Limits to display a list where you can restrict use by day/hour blocking

5. Access to Games is by rating. All games supplied with Windows 7 are rated acceptable to all users

6. You may choose to block particular programs, such as Messenger, Skype, or even Internet Explorer

**Hot tip**

When you choose to block specific programs, you will be presented with the list of programs on your PC. You will have to use the Browse option to locate Internet Explorer and games you have added.

# Windows Live Family Safety

Windows Live Family Safety is included as part of Windows Live Essentials, and must be downloaded before use. It can be used to restrict access to undesirable websites, and to monitor computer usage for all users registered.

**1** Select Start and type Family Safety in the Search box, then click the link that appears. Sign in or register on the Family Safety website

**2** Users with their own Windows account will be listed. Select the account to monitor and click Save

**3** You will be prompted to add passwords for accounts that are currently not password protected. Click the link to Add passwords, if required. Click Next

**4** In the Customize settings for your family, click the link to visit the Family Safety website

Customize settings for your family

Parents can approve or block websites and contacts, and get online activity reports on the Family Safety website.

Go to the Family Safety website: familysafety.live.com

**5** Family members will be listed and so will the computer on which they are registered. Click Edit settings for the new addition

149

**6** Standard settings are for Web filtering Basic and Activity reporting On. Click on any of the settings links in the left column to make changes

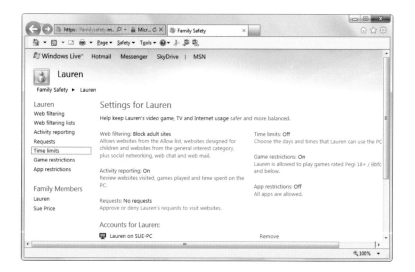

# Online Safety

The Think U Know website, at www.thinkuknow.com/, is an initiative created and managed by the Child Exploitation and Online Protection (CEOP) Centre. The site is co-sponsored by the EU and is a member of the Virtual Global Taskforce, who work to make the Internet a safer place.

The Think U Know website is designed to teach children, between the ages of five and 16, how to use the Internet and latest technology safely. Each age grouping uses a variety of appropriate methods.

The 5-7 age group introduces Hector, a friendly dolphin, to teach basic rules. The site offers a Safety Button which, when clicked, immediately covers the current screen.

1. Select the 5-7 group, click Hector's World and click the Hector's World Safety Button

2. Download and install the relevant version for your operating system

3. Open the Control Panel and click the link to Set up parental controls

**4** Select the user name for the child and, in the More settings area, click Hector's World Safety Button

**5** The next time the child logs on to the PC, they will see a small swimming dolphin. Click the dolphin to hide the current screen

Older children and teenagers will wish to be more adventurous with their Internet use, and may want to spend time on social networking sites. Most sites have ways to report abuse and inappropriate content. Facebook is currently the most popular site and it enhances its privacy settings on an on-going basis. It restricts membership to 13 years and over.

Google offers a Safe Search for children. Visit www.safesearchkids.com/ for a search engine which is

designed to prevent children seeing potentially harmful or illicit information.

**1** Click the link to set the page as the default Home page

**Don't forget**

Parental Controls will be turned on, and Hector's World Safety Button will be activated for that child's user account.

151

**Hot tip**

See Chapter 13 for more on social networking and Facebook.

**Don't forget**

Search engines may generate links to inappropriate sites, unless you apply some form of filtering of the results.

# Early Learning

PBS provides a number of excellent websites for children. To entertain the youngest, visit www.pbskids.org/, where you'll find shows, games and videos targeted at the pre-school age.

The main list of activities uses a voice to introduce the topics, so even non-readers can select a program.

**1** Move the mouse over the arrows to rotate the dial and move over a show icon to hear the title

**2** Select Sesame Street for games, videos, printables (coloring pages, bookmarks etc) and e-cards

**3** Scroll down and play tunes on the hanging chimes, or click a chime to display that character

Encourage a degree of concentration with a program, such as some of those offered on the Nick Junior website at www.nickjr.com, the home of Dora the Explorer, a children's favorite.

1. Open the website and scroll down to the Grown Ups tab and click Menu

2. Select FunFinder and use the filter to select games suitable for the child's age and ability

3. The chosen game will indicate the developmental skills involved. Games have voice direction and narration and make many encouraging comments

153

**Beware**

The Nick Junior website has bases in the US and the UK. You will be redirected to your home country website.

**Hot tip**

The site is commercial, although not overtly so. You are able to buy items from the shop or just sign up for a free newsletter.

# Familiar Names

Children often prefer the familiar, so may welcome the opportunity to play and learn online with well known names from books they have read. For example, the Mr. Men official website at www.mrmenshow.com/us introduces all the Mr. Men (and Little Miss) characters by name.

**Don't forget**

If you are outside the US, you can Select a Country and choose a more local website.

**Hot tip**

The site allows you to turn off the background music without affecting the characters ability to speak.

**1** Click on any character to open their particular web page, where you can choose their game. The games are different for each personality and require differing degrees of concentration and mouse skills

**2** Alternatively, children can watch a video involving the chosen character or select 'free stuff', which includes a downloadable image for use as desktop wallpaper

**Hot tip**

The Pinball game plays in a small window, to maximise the video effects. It has sound effects that youngsters will appreciate.

**3** Older children will love the Pinball game. It uses the arrow keys to fire the ball and manage the paddles

Fisher-Price, the toy maker, offers activities for infant, toddler and preschool age children on their website at www.fisher-price.com

1 Select Games and Activities, Online Games to view the full range. The games are easy to play, but will need adult assistance

Another website that children will be keen to visit is Lego's website, at http://www.lego.com. This site offers a variety of activities to keep children entertained.

1 Choose Games and then browse the sets of games offered. The Action games are designed for older children, with somewhat complicated instructions

2 The Creative section offers several design activities, which may require you to download specific software

3 You can encourage the child to sign in to the free Lego Club. This allows them to save game scores, enter designs into contests and post messages

**Hot tip**

Fisher-Price offers information about child development through play, and parenting advice from experts. In the US, they even offer a newsletter for grandparents.

**Hot tip**

Before introducing children to this website, have a look at some of the games, so that you will be familiar with how they work. You will find it easier to help the child get started.

**Hot tip**

Joining the Lego Club is a way of introducing a child to the concept of an ID and password.

# Basic Skills

When grandchildren come to stay, help them practice their arithmetic, or literacy skills, by playing educational games such as those offered by Knowledge Adventure. This offers a range of math, word, reading, spelling, science and animal games for various ages.

 Type www.knowledgeadventure.com and explore the games by age group, subject or category

If you want to help a child begin or improve reading ability, there are websites that specialize in this area. For example:

 Go to www.starfall.com, a free public service designed to motivate children to read with phonics

**Hot tip**

Select an area such as Grade, then a sub-category such as First Grade Games, to display the relevant subset of the many games available on the website.

**Don't forget**

Visit the Download Center to obtain ABC printouts, reading and writing journals, learn-to-read books, and phonetics puzzle activities.

# Homework Help

Yahoo! Kids website, at http://kids.yahoo.com, provides reference material suitable for children aged six to 12.

1 Click StudyZone tab to focus on academic content

**Hot tip**

StudyZone separates the educational from the entertainment material, so children can study without distractions.

2 Choose a topic or select the searchable World Factbook

3 Alternatively, scroll down to the Directory for links to over 10,000 websites that you can browse or search

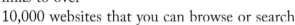

**Don't forget**

Editors review and select everything, and these websites are described as kid-safe and suitable for youngsters to browse.

157

4 Click Reference for the Columbia University Press Encyclopedia and American Heritage Dictionary

# Learn to Type

## Don't forget

The Learn 2 Type website is intended for adults, but there are special sections for children and for schools.

Although using the Internet mainly involves the mouse with point and click, being able to use the correct fingering on the keyboard can be a real asset any user, child or adult.

**1** Type kids.learn2type.com into the browser address bar and select the Sign Up button

## Don't forget

There's a typing test and an interactive typing tutor which automatically adjusts to the child's skill level.

**2** For younger children, there's an easy introduction to typing at www.learn2type.com/tots

## Hot tip

At RapidTyping you can take an online typing test, and download the Typing Tutor for Windows, to practice typing on your computer (no need to be connected).

**3** To improve your skills go to www. rapidtyping. com and click RapidTyping then Download RapidTyping

# Art Appreciation

Broaden your grandchild's horizons by introducing them to art through museums and galleries.

**1** The National Gallery of Art has an interactive website for children at www.nga.gov/kids/

**2** The Metropolitan Museum of Art offers the website www.metmuseum.org/learn/for-kids
Explore the Timeline, or search for the Interactives for kids

**3** If you can't visit in person, go to www. meetmeat thecorner.org/ episodes and select Museum Curator at the MMA

**Hot tip**

Faces & Places, for example, encourages children to create paintings in the style of American native artists, by combining visual elements from more than 100 works from the Gallery's permanent collection.

**Hot tip**

The Heilbrunn Timeline is a chronological, geographical, and thematic exploration of the history of art from around the world, as illustrated by the Museum's collection.

**Hot tip**

This is a video that gives a virtual field trip to the museum, to learn about the work of a curator.

# Foreign Languages

If you would like to help the grandchildren practice a foreign language, or want to brush up your vocabulary or grammar, there are many websites that provide free lessons.

On several language websites you'll find links to Babbel. This website offers free language lessons and is supported by the European Union.

**1** You'll find interactive courses in twelve different languages at www.busuu.com

**2** The Open Culture site at www.openculture.com/ freelanguagelessons has hundreds of links to free language courses, many available through iTunes

## Don't forget

You will need to download iTunes to your PC to view the lessons. A link is provided on the website.

**3** There are links to free courses for about 120 different languages at www.word2word.com You'll also find links to dictionaries and translation services at this site

# Science

Science websites for children are plentiful and excellent, and a good place to start is the NASA site www.nasa.gov
This is, as would be expected, a wonderful resource on space, the solar system and exploration.

**Don't forget**

The NASA Kids Club offers games graded by skill level. Access the site from the Student's page.

**1** From the home page, select For Students. Choose a suitable grade/age for information and games

There are many science museum websites throughout the world, for example the South Kensington London, Science Museum website, www.sciencemuseum.org.uk

**2** Select Online Science, and explore by subjects, museum objects, news items or through games

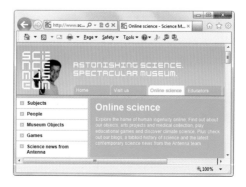

**3** Read the latest science news on the Antenna tab

**Hot tip**

Subjects range from Art to Transport and the articles vary in approach and length but are easy to read, well illustrated and suitable for most ages.

# Understand and Play Music

Children can have great fun learning about music with the San Francisco Symphony.

1   Type the website www.sfskids.org/ into the address bar

2   Click Skip to bypass the Intro music

3   Choose the option Instruments of the Orchestra

4   Select a family of instruments to view and listen to the sound of each individual instrument

5   Alternatively, select the Music Lab, where you learn about tempo, rhythm, pitch and harmony

6   Choose Instrumentation, where you select different instruments and hear how they affect a composition

# Explore the World

The National Geographic website provides authoritative information at www.nationalgeographic.com

**1**    Click the Education tab, and then Students to find resources, maps and topics specifically for students

**2**    Use Encyclopedia Quick Find for specific topics. Matching entries are displayed with a choice of activities or multimedia presentations and the suitable age/grade range indicated

**3**    The Kids link has illustrated topics with a targeted dictionary supporting the information presented

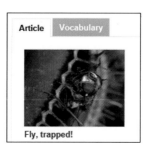

**Don't forget**

Click Connect with us and sign up to a monthly newsletter. You can also follow the news from the National Geographic on Facebook and Twitter.

163

**Hot tip**

The website offers interactive mapping, where you can zoom in to add your own markers.

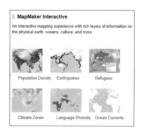

# Help with Revision

There are many websites to help the grandchildren with their revision. The older child can use search engines such as Google, but here are some specific sites to get them started.

## Don't forget

You should make sure that safe search features are turned on in the search engines (see page 149).

1 Go to www.highschoolace.com for lists of free educational resources, arranged in categories

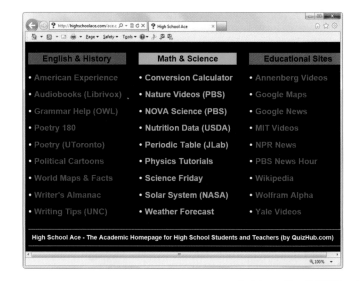

| English & History | Math & Science | Educational Sites |
|---|---|---|
| • American Experience | • Conversion Calculator | • Annenberg Videos |
| • Audiobooks (Librivox) | • Nature Videos (PBS) | • Google Maps |
| • Grammar Help (OWL) | • NOVA Science (PBS) | • Google News |
| • Poetry 180 | • Nutrition Data (USDA) | • MIT Videos |
| • Poetry (UToronto) | • Periodic Table (JLab) | • NPR News |
| • Political Cartoons | • Physics Tutorials | • PBS News Hour |
| • World Maps & Facts | • Science Friday | • Wikipedia |
| • Writer's Almanac | • Solar System (NASA) | • Wolfram Alpha |
| • Writing Tips (UNC) | • Weather Forecast | • Yale Videos |

High School Ace - The Academic Homepage for High School Students and Teachers (by QuizHub.com)

## Don't forget

The BBC offers a vast array of educational websites, from Key Stage graded material to online language courses.

2 Yahoo! has preselected many appropriate references at dir. yahoo.com/education/k_12 There are 11 subject categories and lists of Additional categories covering topics such as distance learning and home schooling

3 In the UK you could choose Bitesize at www.bbc.co.uk/bitesize This is a collection of web pages, purposely designed to encourage revision in manageable sessions

# 11 Keep in Touch

*Whether you are at home or on holiday, the Internet helps you to keep in touch with your family and friends. You can send and receive email, exchange instant messages, or send electronic greetings. With a webcam and software, such as Skype, you can even see one another online.*

# Email Communication

The Internet allows you to communicate with friends, family and business contacts quickly and easily, whether they are just down the street or on the other side of the world. You can send to individuals, or whole groups of people, such as club members, with a simple click of the mouse button. You can include photographs with your email, and attach all kinds of documents, such as Minutes, Agendas and Reports.

Email requires two things – software that allows you to create, save, send and receive messages, and an Internet connection.

### Email Software

Microsoft's Outlook and Windows Live Mail can both be used for email. They are programs that are associated with Microsoft Office and Windows, respectively. Outlook is a full Personal Information Manager, which includes an email program. Windows Live Mail has a subset of Outlook functions.

However, many Internet Service Providers offer their own email facility. They allow you to create, send, receive, read and store your email on their server, using your browser. This is known as Webmail, or sometimes Netmail. Its big advantage is that you can access your mail from anywhere in the world – from a friend's PC, a hotel or an Internet cafe. It does, however, mean that you must be online when using it.

### Web-based email

Each individual ISP offers its own mailbox structure, but they are all very similar in approach. If you are accustomed to using Outlook or Windows Live Mail, the transition to a web-based facility is very straightforward.

Some email accounts are normally web-based only, for example Gmail, Hotmail and Yahoo! mail. For the purposes of this book, we will be using Yahoo! mail.

# Create a Webmail Account

Your ISP may already provide you with a webmail account. However, if you need a new account you can create one at Yahoo.com:

**1** Go to website www.yahoo.com, move the mouse pointer over Yahoo! Mail, then click Sign up

**2** Enter your details. Select one of the suggested IDs, or try your preferred user name, and complete the details. Yahoo! indicates the password strength

**3** Now click Create My Account to get started

**Don't forget**

If you already have a Yahoo! ID, you can sign in with that. You can also sign in using an existing Facebook or Google ID.

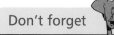

**Don't forget**

The verification process is used to prevent automated registrations. You must be able to read the monitor to type in the letters – something that can only be achieved with the human eye.

167

# Access your Mail

With your mail account now set up, go to www.yahoo.com and sign in. The Yahoo! mail screen opens on the Home tab, which provides current news.

The left panel of the Yahoo! home screen provides quick links to websites associated with or promoted by Yahoo!.

The Mail link shows the number of unopened and recently-received email messages.

**1** Click the Mail button and select View All Yahoo! Mail to open the Mail window

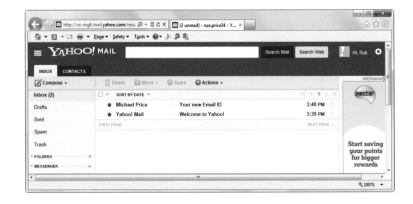

**2** Storage folders are displayed on the left and messages are listed in date received order

## Beware

The Yahoo! mail sign-in screen offers the option to remember your password. This is fine in a domestic situation, but do not select it on anyone else's PC, or in an Internet cafe. See also page 218 (delete browsing history).

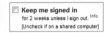

## Hot tip

Click the checkbox next to each message in the Inbox to select it. You can select multiple messages and then click Delete, Spam, etc.

# The Webmail Window

The Folders panel, displays your current folders and enables you to organize your mail.

- the Inbox is where your mail arrives. Messages are immediately displayed when you open the Mail window

- Drafts is where you will store any incomplete messages, or ones that you do not want to send immediately

- the Sent folder keeps a copy of email sent

- the Spam folder will contain any messages that the Yahoo! spamguard program isolates as unwanted

- Trash contains any messages that are no longer required

- the Contacts tab gives you access to your Contact list

**Don't forget**

Spam is the term applied to unwanted, unsolicited and inappropriate messages. Yahoo! provides a Spamguard program to scan emails for such messages, and it is automatically switched on when you sign up with a new ID.

1 Select a message to open it. It opens on a new tab

2 Use the options to Reply or Forward the email

3 Delete, mark as Spam or Move to another folder to remove messages from the Inbox

4 Choose the Previous or Next buttons to move quickly through your messages

**Don't forget**

Click the Inbox tab to close the message and return to the list of messages.

# Create and Send Mail

1 Click Compose on the Mail window to create a new message. The New Message window opens on a new tab

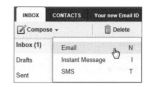

2 Type the recipient's address. If they are in your Contact list, their address or possible matching addresses will be offered for you to select

3 You can insert the address for more than one recipient (+), and can also send Carbon Copies (CCs) and Blind Carbon Copies (BCCs)

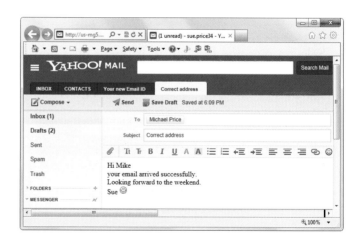

4 Press the Tab key, or click in the Subject box, and type in the topic of the email

5 Tab again to the message area, which offers standard word processing tools, such as font styles and spell checking. Type your message and click Send

6 You get confirmation that the message has been sent. Click Close (X) on the tab to return to the Inbox

# Manage your Mail

Webmail ISPs allocate you storage space on their servers when you sign up for their email facility. Yahoo!, for example, now gives you unlimited storage, as long as you abide by normal email rules and do not abuse the system.

## Sort your messages

**1** Click Date to sort your messages newest to oldest or again to sort in reverse order

**2** Use the other Sort by options to rearrange the listing order and access particular emails more swiftly

171

Hot tip

Sort your messages, newest to oldest, to have your new email appear at the top of the Inbox.

## Manage your messages

**1** Click in the box to the left of the message to select it (insert a tick). Click again to remove the tick. Tick the box next to Sort by, to select by message type

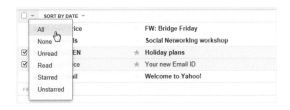

Hot tip

You can tick as many messages at a time as you wish. The messages can then be managed as one.

## Delete your messages

**1** Click Delete to transfer all selected messages to the Trash folder. Messages in the Trash folder do not count towards your total storage

Don't forget

Messages will remain in the Trash folder, allowing you to reinstate them if necessary. Click on Empty to empty the Trash folder.

# Create and Use Folders

To create folders for webmail storage:

**1** Click **+**, next to Folders in the side panel, and type the folder name in the new window

**2** The new folder replaces the Inbox tab as the current view. Click back on the Inbox in the folder list to return to it

**3** The next time you click the Move button, you will have the option to move selected items to the new folder

**4** You can also drag and drop a message into a folder

**5** To rename or delete a folder, right-click the folder and choose the required option. There are also options to empty the Spam or Trash folders

**6** Click the arrow next to Folders to Show your list of folders

**7** Click the arrow again to Hide folders

# Webmail Options

Customize your webmail account and take advantage of features offered by your ISP, using Options on the main Mail window and selecting Mail Options.

1. On the General tab, customize how you view, read and send your messages

173

2. Scroll down to check the Spam settings. SpamGuard is on when you sign up to Yahoo!. Use the Spam Protection options to change settings, such as how long to keep spam messages and where to move allowed messages

3. Click Blocked Addresses and enter addresses that you do not wish to contact you

4. Use Filters to automatically move messages into appropriate folders as they arrive

# Attachments

You can attach documents and photos to the messages you send using your webmail account.

**1** Create your email in the usual way and click the Attach button to locate attachments for the message

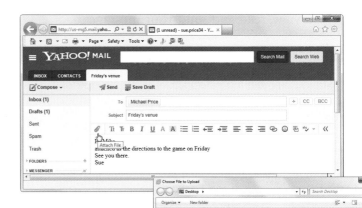

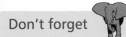
**174**

**2** Navigate your PC's folders to locate and select the required file. Click Open. Repeat to attach more files

**3** The attached file and file size is indicated on the message

**4** Complete your email and then click Send

**5** If you change your mind about a file, click Remove before you send the message

# Receive Attachments

When you receive a file with an attachment:

**1** Check that you know the sender. If you are unsure of the source, then be on your guard

**2** Open the message – the attachment will be indicated in the email header area

**3** Click Save to computer. The attachment is immediately scanned for viruses

**4** You can then select to Open or Save the attachment. Normally you would select Save and then choose the appropriate folder if necessary

**5** The message will be saved into your Downloads folder. Open the folder and move the attachment to its required folder

**Beware**

You should always scan attachments for viruses, even if you know the sender. Yahoo! webmail provides a virus scanner. Check your provider to see what it offers.

175

**Don't forget**

Click Open to view the attachment before downloading.

**Hot tip**

Files are automatically saved into the Downloads folder. Click the arrow next to Save and choose Save As to locate a different destination folder.

# eCards

You can send all kinds of free greeting cards to friends and family using the Internet. Search for a website, for example:

 Go to www. google.com and search for free ecards online

Beware

Some sites may sell on your email details, so make sure there is a reasonable privacy policy in operation.

**2** Choose a category, select a card from those shown and provide the email and message details desired

## E-postcards

Check the website for your holiday destination to see if free digital postcards are offered. For example:

Don't forget

Your recipient will need to stay online to view your ecard or epostcard, unlike your regular email, which they can normally download to their PC.

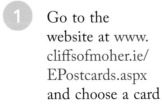 Go to the website at www. cliffsofmoher.ie/ EPostcards.aspx and choose a card to send

# Instant Messaging

Many ISPs and other software companies provide Instant Messaging services. This service allows you to communicate with a selected list of contacts, either by typing your message or by voice. Attach a camera to your PC, and you can even transmit (and receive) video.

For this, you will need to download and install special software. In this example we shall use Skype, which is available at no charge and provides full video service.

1. Visit www.skype.com and click the Download tab, and then click Get Skype for Windows Desktop

**Don't forget**

You will need a full ADSL (broadband) service to use Instant Messaging with video.

2. Internet Explorer will ask you to confirm the download. Click Run to install the Skype software

**Don't forget**

Select Save to save Skype into your Downloads folder, to install later.

3. Follow the prompts and if preferred, deselect the option to Run Skype when the computer starts

# Sign Up to Skype

When you start Skype for the first time you will need to sign in and create an identity for yourself.

1. Supply your name, email address, personal information such as birth date, Skype name and password. As with the Yahoo! ID, you may need to try several Skype names to find one that's available

2. Continue with the sign-up. When the account is created, Skype checks for video and audio configuration and you can choose to provide a picture of yourself that you would like others to see

3. When the formalities are completed, you will see the Skype window ready for you to get started

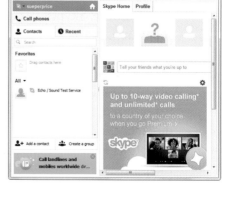

4. Click the Echo/ Test sound service to check that your microphone is working

# Add Contacts

To add Contacts to your Skype account:

**1** Click Contacts, Import Contacts. Skype offers links to social networking sites such as Facebook or your own Outlook address book as a source of Contacts

**Hot tip**

You'd need to enter your Facebook username and password to import your contact list.

Skype searches the address book and lists entries that it recognizes as having a Skype account. Repeat this process for the contacts in any other email or networking service that you use.

**2** If you know someone who has a Skype account, then search the Skype directory. Click Contacts, Add Contact, Search Skype Directory. Enter the person's name, email address or username and Skype will list matching entries

Your contacts must accept your invitation to join your list and vice-versa when they invite you to join.

**Don't forget**

Your can choose which contacts to display, by using the Contacts menu. For example, if you wish to see only those contacts who are online, or only Facebook contacts.

# Make a Call

**1** To connect with a friend, select their name and click on the Call (green phone) or the Video Call button

**2** You'll hear a ringing tone. If your friend is online they will be informed that you are calling. If they are off-line, you will get an automated response to that effect

**3** If the call is accepted, you can type instant messages, have a live conversation (using your microphone) or have a video session (using your web camera)

**4** Click the Video button to turn video display on or off. Click the End Call (red phone) button to terminate the conversation

**5** If your call goes unanswered, you can leave a typed or voice message which your contact can receive on their return

## Status settings

Your contacts will be able to see if you are online. To change your status, click the small tick on the Status bar and select a different option, especially if you don't wish to be interrupted.

# 12 Publish on the Internet

Make files available to other users with storage on the Internet, such as SkyDrive . Create your own website, and let other web users visit your web pages. If you represent a non-profit or volunteer group, set up a website to promote their activities.

# Access Microsoft SkyDrive

Microsoft SkyDrive is a file hosting service that uploads and syncs files to cloud storage and allows access from a Web browser or from your computer. You can keep the files private, share them with contacts or make them public.

To access SkyDrive, you need a Microsoft account.

**1**    Go to www.skydrive.com to initiate access

**2**    If you already have a Microsoft account, enter the email address and password and click Sign in

**3**    Otherwise, enter an existing email address, assign a password for the Microsoft account and enter name, date of birth and other details

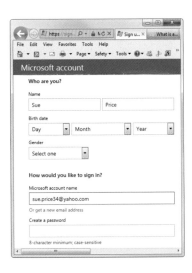

**4**    Click I accept, and reply to the email that you'll receive, then your account is created and you will be signed in

**5** When you are signed in, your SkyDrive is displayed, showing your allowance of 7GB free storage

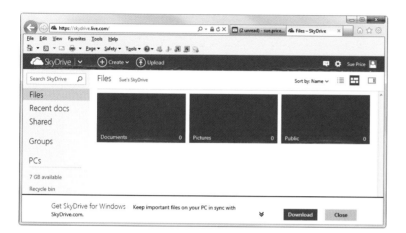

**Hot tip**

While uploading pictures you can keep their original resolutions or choose to resize to save space.

**6** Select a folder and click Upload to copy files from your PC.
Use drag and drop, or select from Windows Explorer

**7** To copy back to the PC, select files or folders in SkyDrive then click the Download button

**Don't forget**

You can Upload files to SkyDrive, then sign on to another PC and Download selected files. The SkyDrive for Windows app (see page 184) does this automatically for all your SkyDrive files.

**8** Folders and multiple files are zipped before transfer

**9** Select Save to copy the file or Zipped files to the Downloads folder on the PC

# SkyDrive for Windows App

Hot tip

SkyDrive for Windows
creates a SkyDrive
on your PC. Files you
put in this folder are
automatically kept
in sync on your PC
and on SkyDrive.com,
so you can access
your latest files from
virtually anywhere.

1 The first time you sign in at www.skydrive.com you
see an invitation to Get SkyDrive for Windows

2 Select Download or leave
this until later, and select Get
SkyDrive applications from
the list on the left

3 You'll see a variety of devices
listed. For a Windows 7 PC select Windows desktop

4 Click Download now then Run to install the app

Don't forget

SkyDrive for Windows
can be installed on PCs
running for Windows
Vista, Windows 7 or
Windows 8.

5 The app is downloaded
and installed on your PC

**6** When the SkyDrive app starts up, follow the prompts to sign in with your Microsoft account

**7** Your SkyDrive is added to Favorites in Explorer

**8** Sync all files and folders or Choose folders to sync

**9** The files are copied from the Cloud to your PC

# Share SkyDrive Files

**1** From SkyDrive on your PC, right-click the folder you want to share and select SkyDrive, Share

**2** Alternatively, sign in to SkyDrive.com, select the folder and click the Sharing button that appears

**3** If it's a library folder such as Documents, you'll get a warning

**4** Enter the email address, add a message, allow Edit if desired, and Require everyone to sign in, then click the Share button

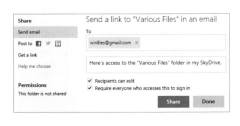

**5** The requested permission will be assigned, and an email notification is sent

6 The invitation to access the files will be sent to the specified email address, with the message displayed and the shared files listed

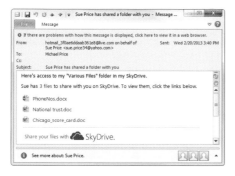

Hot tip

Select an individual file name to view or edit that file using the appropriate web app (see page 188).

7 Select the Files link to access the shared SkyDrive folder, and sign in with your Microsoft account

187

8 You can view the shared folder and its files in the sharer's SkyDrive at the SkyDrive.com website

9 Navigate up and you also have access to Public files

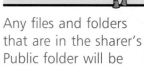
Don't forget

Any files and folders that are in the sharer's Public folder will be available for access even if not specifically offered for sharing.

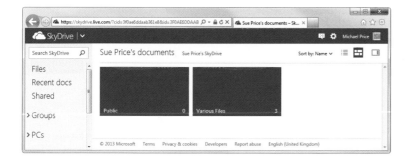

# Edit or Create SkyDrive Files

 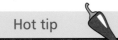
You can work with your SkyDrive files at the SkyDrive.com website. To see the options that are offered:

**1** Sign on to your SkyDrive and open the folder

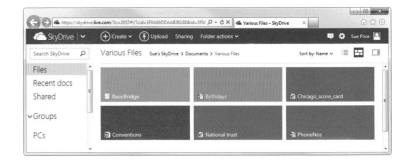

**2** Right-click one of the file types in the folder

**3** Select a file of a particular type and right-click it

- xlsx  — Open in Excel web app or in Excel
- docx  — Open in Word web app or in Word
- pdf   — Open in Internet Explorer

There's a similar choice of web app or local Office program for PowerPoint files and for OneNote files. Other files such as plain text files have no website processing options.

Files of all types can, of course, be downloaded and handled locally on your PC.

You can also create folders and files of particular types directly in your SkyDrive:

**1** Open the appropriate folder, click the Create button and choose an option, for example a Word document

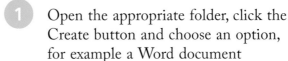

**2** The appropriate web app opens, and you can begin creating your document, using options similar to those provided by the PC based version of the app

**Don't forget**

When you share SkyDrive files, other users can access the documents using the web apps, even if they do not have Microsoft Office installed on their systems.

The Microsoft Word web app lets you make basic edits and formatting changes to your document in your web browser. However, there are limitations to be aware of. For example:

- Word macros cannot be run
- Does not display rulers and gridlines
- Cannot open documents encrypted with a password
- Cannot open file formats .rtf, .html or .pdf
- The Find and Replace function is not supported
- Cannot save in Word 97-2003.doc format

**Hot tip**

There are similar issues with the other web apps, and again you can switch to the PC version to overcome the limitations.

**3** To overcome this and to use more advanced features, select Open in Word to use the version on your PC

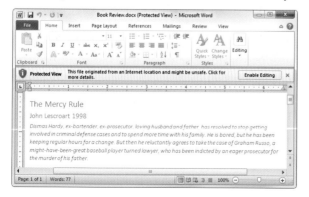

**Don't forget**

When you save the document in Word, it is saved on the website where you originally opened it in the Word Web app.

**Don't forget**

A website of your own provides an alternative to using social networking to communicate with your friends or fellow enthusiasts.

**Hot tip**

You do not need to be an Internet programmer to build a website, and it needn't cost anything at all. However, if you aren't charged a fee, you may find adverts or links added to your web pages.

# Build a Website

If you have something to share, why not create your own pages on the Web? Think of things you might want to publish in your website. It doesn't have to be for business. It could be just for fun, so you can learn first hand about the way the Internet operates. It might be a place where you store information related to a hobby, or interest, that you'd like to share with others who have the same interests. You might have project reports, how-to guides, book reports, photographs or links to associated web pages.

Whatever you want to put in your website, you will need three main items:

1  Storage space on the Internet to record the text and images that you want to share

2  Tools and facilities to help you assemble and arrange those components into the form of a website

3  An Internet address that you can give to others so that they can view your website

Your Internet Service Provider may make web space available, as part of your Internet account, and provide the addressing needed. They would also provide or recommend suitable tools and techniques for building and publishing your web page. However, often the ISP facilities are limited to a predefined home page that may limit what you are able to achieve. Creating your website at the ISP would also make it harder for you to switch suppliers, if your requirements were to change.

Fortunately, there are many other Internet services that will meet all of the requirements for building web pages. For some, it is their main business and they will require a monthly or annual fee, except, perhaps, for the initial trial period. Others, such as Google, may already be providing other services and will offer web page creation as an additional free feature.

# Find Free Website Services

Website services offering free building and hosting change nature over time. For example, Geocities.com was founded in 1995, and was taken over in 1999 by Yahoo!. Initially it continued to offer free website services. However, in 2009, it was replaced by the fee-based Yahoo! Web Hosting service. To see the range of free services currently offered:

1. Go to Google and search for build a free website

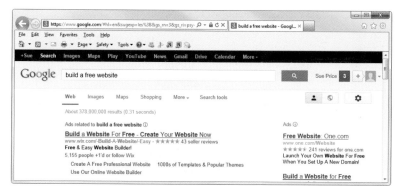

2. You get many millions of matching web pages, and lots of advertisements – free doesn't necessarily mean there's no profit potential, as you'll soon discover

3. Review the services that are listed, to see how they meet your needs, investigating issues such as:
   - The type of website allowed (personal or business)
   - Advertising policy (banners, pop-ups, frames)
   - Amount of web space provided
   - File and web page upload restrictions
   - Use of programming languages, e.g. PHP and Perl
   - Traffic limitations that may be imposed

Scroll down and locate entries that provide "Best of..." lists, for example, the web page with reviews of the Top 10 Free Web Hosting sites (see page 192). This can help you choose the service that will suit you.

the Top 10 Free Web Hosting sites (see page 192).

## Don't forget

While a free website may be ideal for gaining experience, always remember that the service could be withdrawn without notice. Keep backups of your material and have a fall-back plan just in case.

## Hot tip

You should experiment with the services before making your commitment, since some constraints may not be obvious unless you are actively using the systems.

# Review Web Hosting Sites

**1** Locate a web page listing top web hosting sites, e.g. www.prchecker.info/web-hosting/top-10-free-web-hosting-sites

**2** Review the discussion of desirable features, and scroll down for the list of free web hosting services

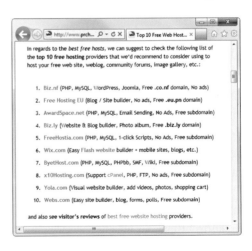

**3** Use this list and other such lists to help you determine which services you would like to try

# Webs (Freewebs)

Webs started out in 2001 as Freewebs, but changed its name in 2008. It provides many facilities for websites, including blogs, forums, calendars, guestbooks, webstores and photo galleries. The basic service is free but there are paid premium services, such as removal of on-site advertisements and the inclusion of more advanced features. To get started:

**1** Go to the website www.webs.com

**2** Enter your email address, choose a password, select your preferred website type then click Get Started

**3** That's all that's needed to create your Webs Account, then you are ready to create your first site

# Set Up your Site

**1** Enter the Site Title that will appear on your website, and choose the specific Site Category

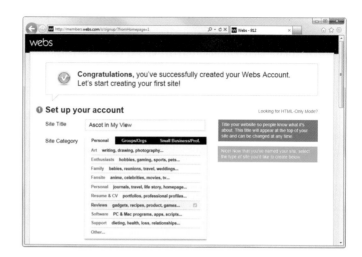

**2** Choose a theme (you can change it later if unsure)

**3** Choose web pages for your site from the recommended and additional pages offered

**1** Agree the terms and click Create My Website

**2** Provide the site address (the subdomain name). If this is checked as Available, click Create My Website

**3** SiteBuilder starts up with a tour of how it works

# Build and Publish your Site

Select any of the modules at the foot of the window then drag & drop to the location on the page where that item is to appear.

**1** Close the tour and SiteBuilder opens your first page with a prompt to start building using drag & drop

Click Pages to insert new web pages. Click Themes to amend the theme settings, and click Dashboard for all the functions needed to manage your website. You can add visitor statistics and even optimize your site for smartphones.

**2** Drag the Title module to add a title for the page, or drag the Image module to add a picture

**3** You can select Upload Image to copy a file from your PC to your website to create a local library of images

# ...cont'd

**4** When you get to the stage where you want to share the details, click Publish

## Hot tip

To stop, click Webs and select Logout. Your progress to date will be saved.

Return to Webs.com and select Sign In to continue editing.

**5** Your pages as defined are copied to the subdomain specified

**6** Click the website link to view your web page on a new tab in the browser

## Don't forget

Click the links to view other pages. Those you've not yet updated will contain just the website Title and sample headings.

# Charity Websites

You can use Webs.com to create and manage a website to support a charitable group or non-profit organization.

**1** Select website type Groups/Orgs and choose a suitable category from the list

If it is a registered charity or other qualifying organization, you may be to able to take advantage of specialist support.

**2** See www. pro-webdesign.biz/free-website-for-charity. html for information on free web design for charities

**3** For help with technical services, go to ServiceSpace at www.servicespace.org/about/team.php

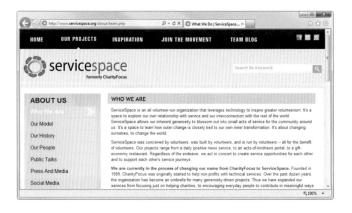

# 13 Social Networking

*Online communities, in the form of blogs and social networks, have become even more popular than email, with online users. Find out what they are, how they work and how to participate.*

# Online Communities

The Internet has created a whole new way of grouping people according to interests, experiences, or activities, in the form of the social networking website.

This type of website creates an online community of Internet users. When you join, you can read the profile pages of other members to get to know about them and you can contact them by instant messaging, telephone or video. You may find the membership is very diverse, being open to individuals from all around the world. You can, however, create your own network of friends within that online community, by locating those who share common interests or goals.

Do proceed with caution when getting to know people online, just as you would when meeting strangers at clubs and bars. By being aware of the potential risks, and using common sense, you should be able to safely participate in and enjoy social networking.

There are hundreds of social networking websites. We discuss a few of the more familiar ones in the next few pages, but you can find a more comprehensive list of active social networking sites at en.wikipedia.org/wiki/List_of_social_networking_websites

**Don't forget**

You are already part of several social networks, the neighborhood, the work place, or your club, for example.

**Beware**

There are dangers associated with social networking, including data theft and viruses. The most prevalent danger though, often involves individuals who claim to be someone they are not.

**Hot tip**

This has almost 200 websites, with a brief description and focus, number of members, type of registration and global ranking. Click the name for a detailed review.

| Name | Description/Focus | Date launched | Registered users | Registration | Global Alexa[1] Page ranking |
|---|---|---|---|---|---|
| 43 Things | Goal setting and achievement | 1 January 2005 | 3,000,000[2] | Open | 13,574[3] |
| Academia.edu | Social networking site for academics/researchers | September 2008 | 211,000[4] | Open | 3,872[5] |
| Advogato | Free and open source software developers | 1999 | 13,575[6] | Open | 318,165[7] |
| aNobii | Books | 2006 | | Open | 13,131[8] |
| AsianAvenue | A social network for the Asian American community | 1997 | | Open | 133,043[9] |

# Blogs

People have always kept a daily journal. Samuel Pepys started his in 1659, and is famed for it to this day. Captain Cook kept a journal, as did many politicians. Even the fictional Bridget Jones kept a diary.

Today, everyone can do it, with the aid of the Internet and a web log, usually shortened to blog. This is a website where the entries are dated (and regularly updated) and displayed in reverse order, latest at the top. They have feedback systems to allow readers to add their comments.

Style and taste in blogs vary enormously. To get a flavour of the range, view a variety of blogs.

1. Go to blogsearch.google.com and search on a topic

You will get a list of related blogs, if there are entire blogs dedicated to your topic, plus a selection of individual blog posts that are associated with your topic.

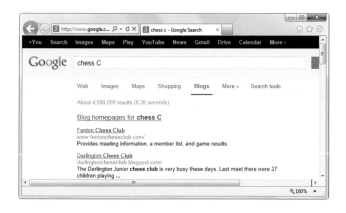

201

## Hot tip

Blogs are perhaps the simplest form of social networking, often related to a particular topic, such as food, politics, or local news.

## Don't forget

The news media and the business world have caught on to blogging, so you will encounter blogs that are commercial in content and purpose. Just skip on to the next in line.

# Create a Blog

## Hot tip

The Internet Explorer Command bar is not currently displayed, to allow maximum screen size whilst creating a blog. See page 18 to restore it.

If you'd like to try blogging, open Google and click the More tab to select Blogger.

**1** Click the link on the Blogger window to Take a quick tour or watch a video tutorial

## Hot tip

You can use an existing gmail or googlemail address, or alternatively click Sign up to create a new account.

**2** Sign in or choose Sign up to set up a new account to proceed

**3** Select your profile type and supply a Display name if using a limited profile

## Hot tip

Initially you may wish to create a limited blogger profile, whilst you learn how blogging works and what the public reaction is to your blogs.

# Post to your Blog

**1** The Dashboard, the main blogging interface, opens ready for you to create your first blog. Click the New Blog button

### Don't forget

The blog address is part of a web address for your blog, so it should be lower case letters, numbers and hyphens only. The address is checked as you type and you are told if the name is available.

**203**

**2** Provide a title for the blog and type in your preferred web address (the URL), then choose a template

**3** Click Create and the blog page is created, ready for your first post. Click the link to Start posting

### Hot tip

You can change or replace the template after your blog has been created, and add features to it.

④ The blog page has text formatting features as in a word processor, including a spell checker

## Hot tip

If you want to add a link to another website, first go to the website and copy its address. Click Link on the menu on the blog window and paste the address where required.

⑤ You can add photos, video clips, links to other websites or email addresses

⑥ Select Preview as you add information to see the layout. Preview opens on a new tab; close the tab to return to the editing page

⑦ Save the page occasionally and click Publish when ready to make it visible at the blog site

## Don't forget

You can use AdSense to display targeted advertising and earn money by promoting suitable products on your blog.

### Other Features
Once you become familiar with the concept of blogging, you can begin to explore extra features available on your blog site. Select the blog title and view the menu offered. You can, for example, edit or remove an individual post. Check the Stats (statistics) to see how many times your pages were viewed or view any Comments that have been made about your blog and decide whether to keep or delete them. Use the template organizer to rearrange the Layout or add a gadget such as a Translate button or video bar.

My blogs

New post
- Overview
- Posts
- Pages
- Comments
- Google+
- Stats
- Earnings
- Layout
- Template
- Settings

# Facebook

Facebook started in 2004 and now has more than one billion active users worldwide. It is open to anyone aged 13 and over. You add friends, and send messages and update your personal profile to tell them what's happening with you. When you add friends they must add you as a friend as well.

1. To join, go to www.facebook.com, provide name, email, password, gender and date of birth, then click Sign Up

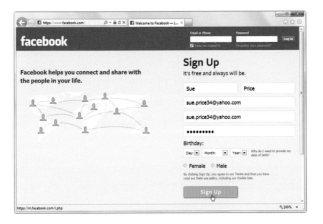

**Don't forget**

Your real date of birth is required to encourage authenticity, but you can hide this from your profile if you wish.

2. Let Facebook search your email address book to locate friends who already have accounts (or ignore this step for the moment and leave the search until later on)

**Hot tip**

If you just want to browse Facebook to start with, you can delay entering your full details until you are more comfortable with the website.

3. Take a Privacy Tour to see what controls are in place and available (see page 207)

# Create a Facebook Profile

## Don't forget

If you want your friends to be able to find you on Facebook, put as much detail as you feel able to share. In particular, put a real photo of yourself, so your friends know it really is you.

**1** Upload a photo of yourself from your computer, or take a photo with your webcam (or skip for now)

**2** To complete your profile click Edit Profile under your photo, adding as much personal detail as you feel is appropriate

## Hot tip

You will receive a Facebook email confirming that the account has been created. Click the link in the message to complete your registration.

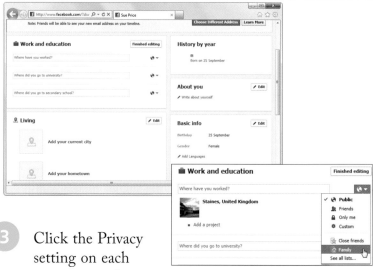

**3** Click the Privacy setting on each category to choose who will be able to see the information you enter

**4** You are now ready to begin searching for contacts

# Facebook Privacy Policy

When you register for a social networking account, you should consider what details and personal information to make generally available. As a guide:

- Information and posts that make it easier for friends to find, identify, and learn about you should be available to Everyone
- The more personal information and details, such as religious and political views, should be restricted to Friends of Friends
- Your contact information, such as mobile phone number and email address, should only be visible to Friends

Until their 18th birthday, minors who use Facebook have their information restricted to Friends of Friends. (See page 147-151 for more on protecting children).

To view and monitor your settings, Facebook has two options:

1 Select the Privacy shortcuts button. Click on any down arrow to expand the view and read about the settings and how the controls are applied

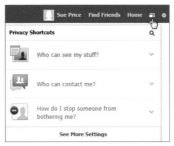

2 Click the Account settings icon to explore both the Security options and the Privacy settings

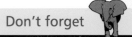

**Don't forget**

Many websites provide links to one another in a form of association. For example, Facebook links to Flickr and Tripadvisor. Facebook also offers to search your Skype, Hotmail and Messenger accounts for friends.

**Hot tip**

Whichever social networking service you decide to join, make sure it offers a suitable privacy policy, so you can protect the information that's important to you.

**Hot tip**

Click Account settings and Log out when you want to leave Facebook completely.

# Twitter

Twitter started in 2006 and now has 500 million active members (*correct at the time of printing*). Its users send and read messages known as tweets. These are text-based posts of up to 140 characters, displayed on the author's profile page and delivered to the author's subscribers, who are known as followers.

Senders can restrict delivery to those in their circle of friends or, by default, allow open access. Users can send and receive tweets via the Twitter website, Short Message Service (SMS), or external applications.

1. Go to www.twitter.com and click Sign up now

2. Follow the prompts to provide your name, username, password, email address and click Create my account

3. Twitter offers a list of Twitter users that you might wish to follow. Select a minimum of five initially

4. Follow the instructions to continue adding names to follow, including those from your own address book, or decide to Skip a step

5. A confirmation email will be sent and you must

Confirm your email address to access all of Twitter's features. A confirmation message was sent to sue.price.ies@email.com.

Resend confirmation   Update email address · Learn more

# Find Someone to Follow

**1** Sign in using your username and your password

**2** Click Discover, Who to follow and type the name of someone you want to follow and click Search Twitter

**3** Select one of the results and check the details, then click Follow. The button changes to Following

**4** Click Home to see the updates they make and their latest tweets. Click in the Tweet box to send your own message

**5** To discontinue following a particular personality or tweet feed, click Me in the menu bar, and click the Following button to Unfollow

# YouTube

YouTube is a video sharing website on which users can upload and share videos. It uses Adobe Flash Video to display a wide variety of user-generated video content, including movie clips, TV clips, and music videos, as well as amateur content, such as video blogging and short original videos. Most of the content on YouTube has been uploaded by individuals, although media corporations, including CBS and the BBC, offer some of their material.

1   To view the videos, go to www.youtube.com

2   There's no need to register or enter personal details, just type the name and keywords into the Search box

3   The results are displayed, in this case a total of six

4   Click the image presented to start the video

# 14 Internet Security

*You need to take care when you visit the Internet, since it has become a target for identity theft. However, there are many ways in which you can protect yourself from risk.*

# Browser Security

Internet Explorer (IE) incorporates a series of enhancements to help protect your system from attackers. These include:

### Automatic Tab Crash Recovery
If a website or add-on causes a tab to hang in IE, that tab is recovered. The browser itself and other tabs are unaffected.

### SmartScreen Filter
This helps protect you from phishing attacks (see page 213), online fraud, spoofed websites and malicious software.

### Add-on Manager
This lets you disable or allow web browser add-ons (see page 214) and delete unwanted ActiveX controls (see page 217).

### Pop-up Blocker
You can limit, or block, most pop-ups (see page 215), choosing the level of blocking you prefer.

### Delete Browsing History
Clear the information stored on your computer when you visit various websites (see page 216).

### InPrivate Browsing and Filtering
This allows you to surf the web without leaving a trail that can be seen, or exploited, by websites or by other users (see page 217).

### Domain Name Highlighting
The domain name in the address bar is highlighted to help you confirm you are visiting a legitimate website.

### Cross-Site Scripting Filter
The CSS filter provides higher security levels to help protect you from hackers and web attacks.

### Windows Defender
IE integrates with Windows Defender to provide live scanning of Web downloads to protect against spyware.

### Parental Controls and Family Safety
IE works with these to provide safer browsing for children.

**Beware**

Your Internet browser is the primary target for malicious individuals or groups, especially identity thieves, who attempt to trick you to steal your personal and financial data.

**Don't forget**

If you should have problems with IE, type Internet Explorer in the Start menu and select the No Add-ons Mode.

🧭 Internet Explorer (No Add-ons)

# Phishing

Internet Explorer has a SmartScreen filter which is designed to operate in the background and to check sites you visit. If it finds suspicious web pages, it displays messages. It also checks the sites you visit against a dynamic list of reported phishing sites. If it finds a match, you get a warning screen. To see it in operation:

**1** Type 207.68.169.170/contoso/enroll_auth.html (a special test website) into the IE address bar and press Enter. You should see the web page illustrated below

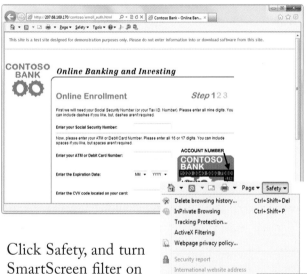

**2** Click Safety, and turn SmartScreen filter on

**3** Confirm that you wish to enable SmartScreen filter and return to the same website, by retyping the address

**4** The same website displays a warning screen

**Hot tip**

Online phishing is a way to trick users into revealing information. It starts with an email that appears to be from a trusted source. Recipients are directed to a fake website, which asks for data, which is then misused.

**213**

**Beware**

Be very sure of the website, before continuing against the advice from the SmartScreen filter.

**Don't forget**

SmartScreen Filter also checks files downloaded from the web and, again, warns you if it finds a match.

# Add-on Manager

If you believe that a new add-on is causing problems on your system, for example generating irritating messages or causing Internet Explorer problems, you can disable it.

**1** Click Tools, Manage Add-ons to view a list of the add-ons installed on your system, (sorted by publisher)

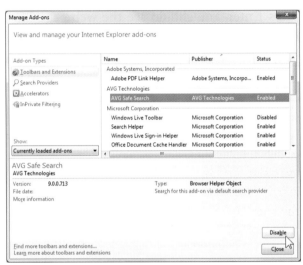

**2** Select the add-on, click Disable, click Close, then restart Internet Explorer

**3** Switching off AVG Safe Search will prevent AVG from checking search results and displaying validations

## Hot tip

Add-ons are small applications that extend the browser (e.g. extra toolbars, animated mouse pointers, stock tickers). Often they come from websites you visit.

## Beware

It is normally sufficient to disable add-ons, and you should not delete them, since it is possible that they may be needed on your system after all.

## Hot tip

To reinstate a disabled add-on, select it as shown and click the Enable button, then click Close and restart the browser.

# Pop-up Blocking

The Pop-up Blocker is turned on in Internet Explorer by default and will block most pop-ups. To try this out:

**1** Visit the website www.popuptest.com, then click to select a test page such as Mouseover PopUp

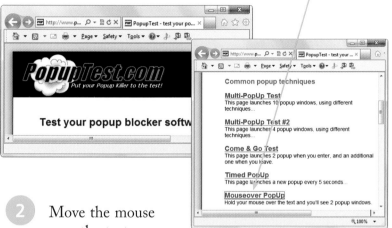

**2** Move the mouse over the text as instructed, and the message Pop-up blocked is displayed on the Information bar at the bottom of the screen

Internet Explorer blocked a pop-up from **www.popuptest.com**.    Allow once    Options for this site ▼    ✕

**3** Click the Information bar and choose to temporarily allow pop-ups at this site (Allow once)

**4** Choose Always allow to have them appear on future visits

**5** Click More options, or if the Information Bar isn't displayed, click Tools, Pop-up Blocker, to display the list of options and to change pop-up blocker settings

# Delete Browsing History

As you browse the Web, Internet Explorer stores details of the websites you visit and data that you type into web forms. The information Internet Explorer stores includes:

## Hot tip

Select Tools, Internet Options and the General tab, to specify Delete browsing history on exit.

- Favorite websites data
- Temporary Internet files
- Cookies
- History of your website visits
- Data entered into web forms
- Saved Passwords

Storing this information is intended to improve your web browsing speed, but you may want to delete the recorded details if you're cleaning up your computer, or if you have been using a public computer.

**1** Click Safety, and then click Delete Browsing History

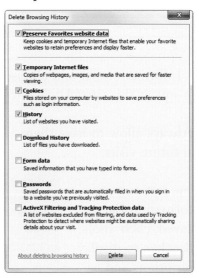

**2** Select, or clear, the boxes to determine which data you want to preserve or delete

## Don't forget

Deleting the browsing history will not delete your list of favorites, or your subscribed feeds.

**3** Click Delete, and then close Internet Explorer when deletion completes, to clear cookies from memory

# InPrivate Browsing/Filtering

InPrivate Browsing prevents Internet Explorer from storing data about your browsing session. This helps prevent anyone else who might be using your computer from seeing where you visited and what you looked at on the Web.

**1** Select Safety, then click InPrivate Browsing

**2** Type the required web address into the Address bar

Tracking Protection helps to prevent websites from collecting information about sites you visit.

**1** Select Safety, then click Tracking Protection

**2** Create your own list or click the option to go online for an up-to-date list of Tracking Protection providers

## Beware

InPrivate Browsing starts in a new window and all tabs in that window are protected. If you open another browser window, that window will not be protected.

## Hot tip

To end InPrivate Browsing, just close the window.

## Don't forget

ActiveX Filtering prevents websites from installing programs or collecting information from your computer. Just click the option to turn it on or off.

# Fix My Settings

You can make changes to your Internet settings that result in your system becoming insecure. For example:

## Hot tip

It may sometimes be necessary to reduce the level of security to install a particular application. This feature makes sure that you do not leave the system in an insecure state.

**1** Click Tools, Internet Options and the Security tab, and click Custom Level. Select an option labelled as not secure

**2** Click OK, then Yes to change the setting

**3** Internet Explorer now displays an Information warning

**4** When you re-open Internet Explorer you are warned that your settings are unsafe

## Don't forget

If Internet Explorer becomes unstable, and you need to restore all settings, click Tools, Internet Options, and the Advanced tab, then click Reset.

**5** Click the Information Bar and select Fix settings for me

**6** Alternatively, click the Settings button for more information. Click Default level to restore the settings. Restart Internet Explorer for the settings to be applied

# Windows Update

**1** Click Control Panel, System and Security, Windows Update (or Start, All Programs, Windows Update)

Hot tip

Windows Update provides you with online updates to keep your computer up-to-date with the latest security fixes.

Don't forget

Click Change Settings and choose Microsoft Update, to receive updates for Office as well as for Windows.

**2** Click the View Update History link to see a list of all the updates that have been applied to your system

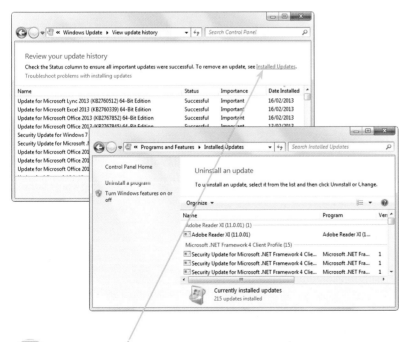

**3** Click Installed Updates to view the important updates and, if necessary, uninstall selected updates

# Firewall and Malware

## Hot tip

When Action Center opens, click the arrow next to System to display the details.

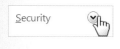

**1** Select Start, Control Panel, System and Security and then Review your computer's status

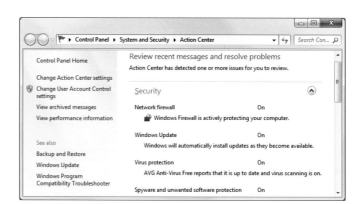

## Don't forget

You need Firewall software to prevent other systems from accessing your computer when you are on the Internet.

**2** Both Firewall and Malware protection should be On

**3** Automatic updating should also be On, if your system is connected via ADSL or Cable

Windows Vista and 7 include built-in Firewall software, along with Windows Defender, to protect against spyware. Windows 8 comes with an updated version of Defender that also includes antivirus software. Also, if no third-party product was supplied with your system, you can download the AVG Free Edition antivirus software from free.avg.com, for personal use, or software from other suppliers, including Symantec, Sophos and McAfee.

## Don't forget

Antivirus software detects any malicious software that may get onto your system. It can prevent or undo any harmful effects.

# Website Directory

*These are websites from across the world that are of particular interest to seniors, to help you continue your exploration of the Internet.*

# 50 Plus Information

### AARP
www.aarp.org

Originally the American Association of Retired Persons, AARP is a nonprofit, nonpartisan membership organization for people aged 50 and over, whether retired or not. US citizenship is not required for membership.

### CARP
www.carp.ca

This is the Canada's association for 50-plus, and it aims to promote the rights and quality of life for mature Canadians.

### Internet Senior Success Center
www.internetseniorsuccess.com/seniorsites.htm

An resource targeting seniors and baby boomers offering links by category, to government departments, magazines etc.

### Silver Surfers
www.silversurfers.net

This was created for the UK, but does have an international flavor. It is an interface to some of the best websites for the over 50s, with links to over 10,000 – British and worldwide.

**Hot tip**

A popular Australian website for the over 50s can be found at http://greypath.com

**Hot tip**

The websites are mainly related to US states and Canadian provinces, plus some international listings.

# Communicating

### Classmates Online      www.classmates.com

Classmates Online connects members
throughout the US and Canada with
friends and acquaintances from school,
work and the military. Its Classmates International
subsidiary operates in Sweden, France, Austria and Germany.

### People Search      www.whowhere.com

If you want to
track down an
acquaintance in the
United States, not
necessarily an old
school or army mate,
this search website
will help you find the latest contact data. You can use it to
also find the name and address for a contact when you have
the phone number.

### Friends Reunited      www.friendsreunited.co.uk

You may be able to locate some of your
old classmates by registering at Friends
Reunited. The site lets you select and make
an entry under your school, university,
club or armed forces for several, mainly
commonwealth, countries.

### Forces Reunited      www.forcesreunited.org.uk

For the British Armed Forces Community, it offers forums,
chat, military news competitions, genealogy and access to
discounts for the military. You do not have to have served in
the armed forces to join.

# Digital Photography

### Photographic Walks          www.all-free-photos.com

A collection of over 2,500 high resolution images of European walks and travels, in galleries of castles and parks, towns and villages, landscapes and panoramic views.

### Tips              www.digital-photography-tips.net

The site contains articles, tutorials, help with choosing a digital camera, a glossary and much more. Difficult scenarios, such as low light and night photography, are covered.

### More Tips            www.internetbrothers.com

Visit the PhotoTips page at the Internet Brothers website for another selection of digital photography tips and tutorials. For example, there is a step-by-step guide on how to take a series of overlapping digital photos and turn them into a 360° panorama video.

**Internet Brothers**
HELPWARE FOR THE CYBERCOMMUNITY

# Learning

## OpenLearn      www.open.ac.uk/openlearn

A learning resource from the Open
University. The site is available to anyone,
anywhere in the world. The source
material comes from the Open University, is designed for
distance learning and is free. OpenLearn is principally
for informal study. You do not need to register, but it is
recommended that you do.

**Don't forget**

OpenLearn does
not grant awards or
credits, require you
to become an Open
University student or
offer tutorial support.

## Online University      www.education-portal.com

Search for the article titled Colleges and Universities that
Offer Free Courses Online, for a list of institutions that have
decided to make course materials, including lectures, tests,
notes and readings, available for free on the Internet.

**Hot tip**

The list includes world-
class institutions like
MIT, Stanford, Yale and
UC-Berkeley.

## Online School      www.free-ed.net

Free-Ed.Net is an online
school that offers nearly 200
career and academic courses.
Normally, there is no sign-up
and there is no cost to you. However, Free-Ed cannot offer
diplomas or certificates of completion.

## TED      www.ted.com

A non-profit organization devoted to Ideas Worth
Spreading. Originally for Technology, Entertainment and
Design, its scope now includes global issues, business and
science. It offers fascinating talks by
well known people, and is free.

**Don't forget**

You can get TED talks
with RSS Feeds. They
are currently translated
into 63 languages.

...cont'd

Hot tip

Road Scholar, operated by Elderhostel promises behind-the-scenes and in-depth experiences for its cultural tours and study cruises.

### Road Scholar    www.roadscholar.org

This is a not-for-profit educational travel organization, providing opportunities for international travel, with 6,500 offerings a year in more than 150 countries.

### SeniorNet    www.seniornet.org

SeniorNet is aimed at computer-using adults, age 50 and older. It supports over 240 Learning Centres throughout the US and in other countries, publishes newsletters and instructional materials, and offers online e-courses on a variety of subjects.

### U3A    www.harrowu3a.co.uk/u3a_sites.html

U3A (University of the Third Age) is an international organization whose aims are the education and stimulation of retired members of the community. The Harrow U3A maintains a list, by country, of links to U3A worldwide and other institutes for learning in retirement.

Don't forget

If you have skills and knowledge in any area, U3A gives you the opportunity to teach others and share your expertise.

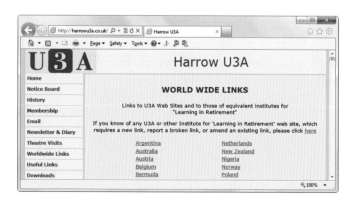

# For Children

## How Stuff Works    www.howstuffworks.com

A subsidiary of Discovery Communications, the site offers information on anything from cosmetics to stem cell research. The website has become a recognized source of easy to understand explanations and also has quizzes and puzzles.

Hot tip

Founded originally by North Carolina State University, the site has won multiple awards.

## Online Art Lessons    www.kinderart.com

KinderArt is a large collection of free online art lessons, ideas and resources which have been contributed by people from around the world.

## Museum of Natural History    www.amnh.org

The American Museum of Natural History website provides help in planning your visits, offers online resources to supplement its special exhibitions and includes a section designed for Kids & Families.

Hot tip

If there's a museum near you, search on the Internet for its associated website.

## Reading and Games    www.seussville.com

If your grandchildren love The Cat in The Hat, go to the Seussville site for some games with the colorful Seussville characters.

# Publishing on the Internet

### Accessibility Initiative
#### www.w3.org/wai/users/browsing

Seniors know better than most how web pages can become unreadable, due to poor color, contrast, etc. This overview summarizes the key concepts of accessible web design (e.g. a site suitable for the visually impaired) as a set of quick tips.

**Hot tip**

In this particular website, the case of the web page address does not matter. If you enter the address as all lowercase it will be adjusted to partial capitalization.

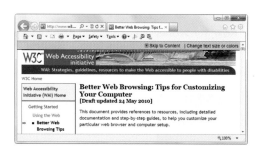

### Piers Anthony    www.hipiers.com/publishing.html

Piers Anthony (the writer of the Xanth fantasy series) and his blog-style survey of Internet publishers may be useful, when you finish that novel you've always meant to write.

**Hot tip**

The website address changes to the current year, for example, 2013.bloggies.com. You can also visit the results for previous years, for example, 2012.bloggies.com.

### Weblog Awards    www.bloggies.com

This website tells you how to nominate weblogs for the various categories, gives details of the judging procedure and lists the finalists and the winning entry for each category.

228

# Reference Material

## GWR — www.guinnessworldrecords.com

Whenever you wonder what's the largest (or any other -est), you'll find the answer at the Guinness World Records site.

## Merck Manual — www.merck.com/pubs

Merck makes available a series of online manuals, including the Merck Manual of Medical Information – Home Edition, which translates complex medical information into plain language. There's also an online Merck Manual of Health & Aging.

## Dictionary — www.thefreedictionary.com

Free to use, this website gives access to a standard English dictionary, as well as medical, legal, financial and 13 foreign language dictionaries. Usefully, it has a compendium of acronyms and one for idioms. There are daily word challenges, and an English language forum. Type a word into the Free Dictionary and search, using its own volumes. Alternatively, click the Google or Bing options to perform a different search with alternative results.

## Encyclopedia — www.encyclopedia.com

This site searches dictionaries and encyclopedia for facts, biographies, word origins, etc. It includes images and newspaper articles in its search results.

## World Airport Codes — world-airport-codes.com

With almost 10,000 listed, this site provides airport codes, abbreviations, runway lengths, location maps and other information for almost every airport in the world.

**Hot tip**

Sources include Columbia and World Encyclopedia, Oxford's World Encyclopedia, and the Encyclopedia of World Biography.

**Don't forget**

You don't always need to enter the full website address, as this example shows.

# Travel

**Hot tip**

You will find similar travel services in other countries, for example the CAA in Canada and AA Travel New Zealand.

**VisaHQ**          www.visahq.com/citizens

This website covers the USA, Canada and the UK. It lists countries alphabetically, lets you select your nationality and then shows whether you need a visa, and if so which type – a visitor, business or official visa.

**Track Flights**          www.flightstats.com

If you know the airline, flight number, departure airport or destination, you can check the flight situation. To track the  actual flight, you will need to log in, then you will get real time positioning, as long as the plane is not over an expanse of water and has agreed to share its data.

**Travel Health**          www.cdc.gov/travel

CDC Travelers' Health offers information to assist travelers and their health-care providers in deciding the vaccines, medications, and  any other measures necessary to prevent illness and injury during international travel. Click the country box to select your destination.

**Don't forget**

Saga also market insurance and finance products, there's a Saga Magazine and a Saga social networking site.

**Saga Holidays**          www.saga.co.uk/holidays.aspx

The Saga Group focuses exclusively on the provision of services for people 50 and over. These include holidays to worldwide destinations, from cruises to self-catering.

# Sport

## Manchester United FC     www.manutd.com

Describing itself as the most popular football club in the world, this website has all the information you could want about the club. Topics include matches, interviews, event lists and video clips of past matches. Sign up (its free) to receive an email newsletter, exclusive information and services.

Hot tip

Information about the Wimbledon Lawn Tennis championships can be found at www.wimbledon.com The tournament is so popular that tickets are only available in a ballot, applied for by the end of December for the following year.

## America's Cup     www.americascup.com

The same type of content, but this time with sailing, is available on the America's cup website. You can join the fan club, or enlist as a volunteer where all kinds of opportunities exist, from office assistant to helicopter spotter.

## US Open Golf     www.usopen.com

Golf enthusiasts can follow the tournaments, buy tickets and again volunteer for events. You can use the site to learn about handicapping, course rating and calculators.

# On-line Utilities

When you are unable to access a particular website, visit www.isup.me. The site checks whether the named website is working or is temporarily unavailable.

When you copy and paste a web address into an email, you may end up with an extended or complex link. Visit www.tinyurl.com for a free website that will make a shorter web address for your link.

Would you like to know who is responsible for or owns a website? Try the website http://whois/ and enter the name of the business. Scroll down to see details such as ownership, server name and registrant.

# Index

239

## X

## Y

## Z